D1356112

Home Winemaking

Ian Ball

Charles Letts & Co Ltd
London Edinburgh and New York
Head Office: Diary House, Borough Road, London SE1 1DW

Contents

By the same author:
Wine Making The Natural Way
Traditional Beer And Cider Making

Both books published by Elliot Right Way Books
in their **Paperfronts** series.

ISBN No: 0 85097 680 4
Log concept: © 1985 Charles Letts & Co Ltd
Text: © 1985 Ian Ball
Illustrations: © 1985 Charles Letts & Co Ltd
Printed in Great Britain by Charles Letts (Scotland) Ltd

How to use the log

Your home-made wines can easily achieve a standard equal to commercial wine. With practice, experiment and careful record-keeping, your wines will far exceed the mediocre quality of many modern mass-produced and mass-marketed table wines. Beer drinkers, too, can find out how beer and ale used to be made, and how to make full flavoured varieties at home for a fraction of the commercial price.

Keeping a winemaking log is the ONLY way to understand fully how and why wines develop, improve and mature to varying degrees of excellence. In your *Letts Log for Winemaking*, you can record details of the way your natural ingredients are skilfully blended and transformed into wine, and your impressions of the wine's progress from cloudy, harsh-tasting liquor to bright, appetizing bottled wine. You will acquire a level of understanding and expertise that will enable you to guarantee near perfection in any wine you produce.

Accurate record-keeping makes possible the precise reproduction of your most popular or adventurous wines. Your records will also help you plan exciting new wine recipes for admiring guests.

The log pages are divided into headed sections to help you note important information in an easy-to-find layout for future reference.

Begin by entering the name of your wine and the date you add wine yeast to the ingredients. List the main natural ingredients and chemicals (if any). The type and amount of pure honey used is particularly important (see page 20) because pure honey, in addition to supplying alcohol content, has a distinctly beneficial effect in the finished wine: each honey bestows unique characteristics of flavour and bouquet (aroma). The quantity of sugar used (if any) gives an idea of the likely alcohol content of the wine.

The 'Remarks' section is for information you consider important. It may include initial and final wine hydrometer readings, or *specific gravities* (see page 24); notes on whether the wine's fermentation (see page 4) was vigorous or slow; air temperatures and/or weather conditions during fermentation and dates on which the wine was poured or syphoned (*racked*) from sediment (see page 40). Simply record the dates, figures and observations you think significant.

Note the date on which you store your fermented wine to clear and mature; the date on which you bottle your clear wine, and describe its final colour. All this information proves useful when comparing wines and analyzing results.

Record the date you open the first bottle of a batch and describe the bouquet, flavour and impression of alcoholic strength. Choose descriptive words or phrases that jog your memory when you refer to the entry, and provide a standard scale for comparison.

Name of wine:	Main ingredients:	Honey used:
Caribbean sunset	Pineapple juice	
Date yeast added: 14 Jan '85	orange juice	Sugar
	White grape juice	
Date wine stored: 12 Feb '85		

Why make wine?

Winemaking is an ancient craft, practised for centuries by country folk. Any non-poisonous natural ingredients can be turned into economical, nourishing wine. The vitamins, minerals and health-giving goodness of natural ingredients are extracted by the winemaking process. For generations our ancestors enjoyed the natural goodness of tasty wines made from honey, herbs, vegetables, fruit and flowers.

Natural wines were among our first medicines. Ancient folk wisdom prescribes blackcurrant wine (brimming with vitamins) as a remedy for sore throats, coughs and colds; coltsfoot wine (rich in vitamin C) as a pleasant cure for coughs and chest complaints; dandelion wine (high in vitamins A, C and B,) as a tonic, blood purifier and guard against colds, rheumatism and anaemia; and mead (made from honey; packed with vitamins, mineral salts and unidentified trace elements) as a rejuvenating aphrodisiac.

Beware! Poisonous plants

For safety's sake, when making your own wines, stick to natural ingredients recommended in tried and tested recipes. Poisonous plants include: anemone, azalea, bluebell, buttercup, clematis, columbine, crocus, crowfoot, cyclamen, daffodil, dahlia, foxglove, all fungi, geranium, gladiolus, hemlock, hyacinth, iris, lobelia, lupin, narcissus, all varieties of nightshade, peony, poppy, rhubarb leaves (leaves only), snowdrop, sweet pea, tobacco, tulip.

Making wine

Wine may be made from pure juices diluted with water and/or whole ingredients soaked in water to extract flavour and colour.

Fruit and pure fruit juice contain natural sugar (fructose and glucose). Flowers and many vegetables have no sugar content. Natural sugar (fructose and glucose) or processed household sugar (sucrose) must be present for wine yeast to convert to alcohol. The action of wine yeast turning sugar to alcohol is called *fermentation*. During fermentation, wine yeast's conversion of sugar to alcohol produces harmless carbon dioxide gas. The gas bubbles up through the fermenting wine and escapes into the air.

The flavour of your wine is decided largely by the principal ingredient, after which the wine is usually named. Also essential to a balanced wine are tannin and acid. Both tannin and acid (either citric, malic, or tartaric acid) occur naturally in some ingredients commonly used for making wines. However, addition of tannin and/or acid is usually necessary in recipes to raise the acid and tannin content to a desirable level. Apart from giving extra taste to wine, tannin and acid play a major part in guarding wine against infection; encourage rapid fermentation of the wine and assist the wine to clear, mature and quickly achieve its full potential.

Recipe guidelines

The recipes in this log give you a format around which to formulate your own recipes. Take care to avoid poisonous ingredients (see left) and if in doubt about the safety of any ingredient, leave it out. Fresh and dried herbs, dried berries, flowers and seeds used in the recipes are available from health food stockists.

To make 1 gallon (4½ litres) of natural wine you require:

Main natural ingredient	Quantity
Pure fruit juice	about 1¾ pints (1 litre)
Pure vegetable juice	about 1¾ pints (1 litre)
Fresh flower petals	from 1¾ pints (1 litre) to 4 pints (2¼ litres)
Dried flower petals	from 2 oz (56 g) to 4 oz (113 g)
Fresh fruit	from 2¼ lb (1 kg) to 4½ lb (2 kg)
Dried fruit	from 1 lb (454 g) to 1½ lb (680 g)
Fresh vegetables	about 4½ lb (2 kg)

* The greater the quantity of main ingredient, the fuller your wine's flavour and texture (or 'body').

Sugar-free winemaking

If you want to make wine free of processed household sugar (sucrose), replace the recommended weight of sucrose in any recipe with an equivalent weight of natural sugar (fructose and glucose) found in selected natural ingredients. The best balance of natural ingredients containing fructose and glucose is a combination of pure honey, grape juice and sultanas (dried white grapes) or raisins (dried black grapes). Currants may also be used. Refer to recipes in this log for examples of the right way to blend these ingredients as a replacement for household sugar.

Natural ingredient	Natural sugar, fructose and glucose content
1 lb (454 g) pure honey	about 14 oz (397 g)
1 pint (568 ml) pure grape juice, red or white	about 4 oz (113 g)
1 pint (568 ml) winemaking concentrated grape juice, red or white	about 16 oz (454 g)
1 lb (454 g) raisins	about 10½ oz (298 g)
1 lb (454 g) sultanas	about 10½ oz (298 g)
1 lb (454 g) currants	about 10½ oz (298 g)

Equipment

To make 1 gallon (4½ litres) of wine, sufficient to fill six standard size wine bottles, you need:

1 One 2¼ gallon (10 litre) plastic (food grade) bucket with lid.
2 One 1 gallon (4½ litre) narrow-necked vessel or *demijohn*, specially manufactured and marketed for winemakers. (Narrow-necked vessels are referred to as 'demijohns' throughout this log.)
3 One bored cork or rubber bung and an air lock or 'fermentation lock'.
4 One solid cork or rubber bung.
5 One 4 ft (1.2 m) length of plastic syphon tubing and plastic on/off tap.
6 Six standard size wine bottles and six cork or plastic stoppers.

Other items of value to the winemaker include: large wooden or plastic spoon for stirring; fine mesh straining bag; plastic funnel with 5 inch (127 mm) or 6 inch (152 mm) diameter mouth; plastic measuring jug; kitchen scales and a bottle brush.

You can make wine with minimum equipment. However, as your experience and expertise grow, you may like to invest in some of the excellent specialist equipment on sale to today's winemaker. Accessories which could be of interest include: hydrometer (see page 24) and trial jar; filter kit for clearing stubbornly cloudy wines; heating pad or belt to keep wine fermenting in cold, wintry conditions; wine testing kit to check for the presence and levels in wine of acid, residual sugar, pectin or starch; a small wine press to crush pure juice from fresh fruit.

Think big

Once you have made and sampled a wide range of natural wines, you may decide to make your favourites in quantities larger than 1 gallon (4½ litres) at a time. It's almost as easy to make 5 gallons (23 litres) as 1 gallon, and the extra bottles of wine help lay the foundation of a very fine 'cellar' of superb natural wines that provide for every social occasion. Large-capacity winemaking buckets, bins and fermentation vessels are available in sizes which hold up to 5½ gallons (25 litres) of wine.

Safety hints

1 Never ferment wine in earthenware or metal containers. Alcohol formed in fermenting wine might draw mildly poisonous chemicals from such containers into your wine.

2 When using plastic vessels to ferment wine, be certain they are suitable for food use, or marketed specifically for home brewing.

Air locks

An air lock, or fermentation lock, slots into the hole bored through a cork or rubber bung. The bung and attached air lock plug into the mouth of your demijohn.

The air lock is then filled with water or sulphite solution (see page 8). Bubbles of carbon dioxide gas resulting from the wine's fermentation pass up through the liquid in your air lock. The air lock protects your wine from infection by airborne bacteria.

When the wine yeast has converted all natural sugar (fructose and glucose) and any household sugar (sucrose) to alcohol, the steady bubbling stops. In this way your air lock indicates that fermentation has finished and the wine is ready to be syphoned or poured (racked) into a vessel to clear and mature before being bottled (see page 40).

Staying in touch

Winemaking equipment is constantly improved and advanced. The surest way to stay abreast of the latest developments is to visit your local homebrew stockist regularly, view the articles on display and seek the advice of the staff on suitable equipment and accessories. Do not forget the monthly winemaking and homebrew magazines available through newsagents.

Most areas of the UK have a Winemakers' Club, Guild or Circle. Many home winemakers gain great enjoyment from joining one of these instructive and helpful groups.

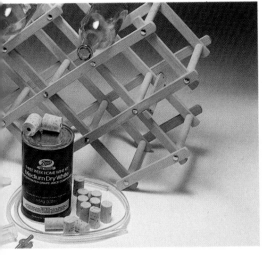

Sterilizing equipment

Kill bacteria! Sterilize all equipment employed at each stage of winemaking and eliminate the chance that bacteria on utensils might infect and ruin your favourite wine.

The most economical way of sterilizing equipment is to prepare a bottle of sulphite solution.

Sulphite solution

Sodium metabisulphite powder (available from homebrew stockists) or	1 oz (28 g)
Campden tablets (available from homebrew stockists)	9 (crushed)
Water, warm	1 pint (568 ml)

Dissolve the sodium metabisulphite powder *or* the crushed Campden tablets in the warm water. Do not breathe the fumes given off when the chemical and water are mixed, as they cause momentary, mild irritation to throat and lungs. Pour the solution into a clean wine bottle and fit a cork or plastic stopper. Your sulphite solution is now ready for immediate use. Simply pour the sulphite solution into cleaned buckets, fermentation vessels, bottles etc; swill it round and then pour back into its bottle and fit the stopper. *Always* rinse away with water traces of sulphite solution from sterilized items *before* using to make wine.

To sterilize the outside of buckets, lids, bottles etc, dip a clean cloth in a saucer of sulphite solution and wipe items. Do not forget to rinse the cloth in water afterwards and then thoroughly rinse the sterilized equipment.

Sulphite solution diminishes in quantity through usage, but remains potent for months and may be used repeatedly.

Air locks

It is wise to put a little sulphite solution in air locks when fermenting wine. The solution has no contact with the wine and guards against possible infection by airborne bacteria. Bacteria can, though seldom do, pass through water in an air lock and infect the wine. Play safe – use sulphite solution.

Stains and moulds

To remove obstinate stains and moulds from bottles, fermentation vessels etc, soak them in warm water and washing-up liquid *or* hot water and a few dissolved household soda crystals *or* diluted or neat household bleach; then scrub clean with a winemakers' bottle brush and rinse well with water before sterilizing with sulphite solution.

A wide range of sterilizing agents that clean and sterilize in one operation are stocked by homebrew suppliers.

Name of wine:	Main ingredients:	Honey used:	Remarks:
Date yeast added:		Sugar:	
Date wine stored:			
			Date first bottle opened:
Date clear:	Chemicals:	Final colour:	Bouquet (aroma):
			Flavour:
Date bottled:			Alcohol (light/med/strong):

9

Name of wine:

Main ingredients:

Honey used:

Remarks:

Date yeast added:

Sugar:

Date wine stored:

Date clear:

Chemicals:

Final colour:

Date first bottle opened:

Bouquet (aroma):

Date bottled:

Flavour:

Alcohol (light/med/strong):

Name of wine:	Main ingredients:	Honey used:	Remarks:
Date yeast added:		Sugar:	
Date wine stored:			
Date clear:	Chemicals:	Final colour:	Date first bottle opened:
Date bottled:			Bouquet (aroma):
			Flavour:
			Alcohol (light/med/strong):

11

Name of wine:	Main ingredients:	Honey used:	Remarks:
Date yeast added:		Sugar:	
Date wine stored:			
Date clear:	Chemicals:	Final colour:	Date first bottle opened:
			Bouquet (aroma):
Date bottled:			Flavour:
			Alcohol (light/med/strong):

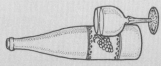

12

Name of wine:	Main ingredients:	Honey used:	Remarks:
		Sugar:	
Date yeast added:			
Date wine stored:			
			Date first bottle opened:
Date clear:	Chemicals:	Final colour:	Bouquet (aroma):
			Flavour:
Date bottled:			Alcohol (light/med/strong):

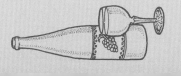

13

Name of wine:

Main ingredients:

Honey used:

Remarks:

Date yeast added:

Sugar:

Date wine stored:

Date clear:

Chemicals:

Final colour:

Date bottled:

Date first bottle opened:

Bouquet (aroma):

Flavour:

Alcohol (light/med/strong):

Name of wine:	Main ingredients:	Honey used:	Remarks:
Date yeast added:		Sugar:	
Date wine stored:			
			Date first bottle opened:
Date clear:	Chemicals:	Final colour:	Bouquet (aroma):
			Flavour:
Date bottled:			Alcohol (light/med/strong):

15

Name of wine:	Main ingredients:	Honey used:	Remarks:
Date yeast added:		Sugar:	
Date wine stored:			Date first bottle opened:
Date clear:	Chemicals:	Final colour:	Bouquet (aroma):
Date bottled:			Flavour:
			Alcohol (light/med/strong):

Key to chemicals

Many chemicals are on sale to today's winemaker. Here is your guide to some of the chemicals available, together with the main beneficial effects their use should have on your wine.

Please follow the manufacturer's directions closely when using a chemical, or you might spoil the quality of your finished wine.

Acid blends (citric, malic, tartaric) For use with wines made from ingredients low in natural acid, particularly flower, grain, leaf and vegetable wines. Adds flavour and guards against infection; speeds fermentation; assists maturation and increases storage life of the wine.

Ammonium phosphate and/or sulphate Encourages strong and rapid growth of yeast in fermenting wine.

Ascorbic acid Anti-oxidant, absorbs excess air admitted to fermented wine when syphoned or poured to a new container or bottled. Also raises the acid level in wine.

Bentonite A natural clay which clears wines.

Campden tablets Contain sodium or potassium metabisulphite. Sterilant and anti-oxidant. Kill bacteria; inhibit development of bacteria and absorb excess air in wine.

Citric acid In its natural form, found mainly in citrus fruits. See 'Acid blends'.

Diammonium phosphate See 'Ammonium phosphate' above.

Fungal amylase Prevents starch haze in grain and vegetable wines when added to ingredients before fermentation, or during the early stages of fermentation.

Glycerol Smoothes harsh taste of fermented wine; rounds flavour and adds silky 'feel'.

Malic acid In its natural form found mainly in apples. See 'Acid blends'.

Nutrient salts Also advertised as 'yeast energizers'. A combination of chemicals offering a range of vitamins to encourage a strong colony of yeast and rapid fermentation of the wine. The main vitamins required for fast yeast growth are B_1 and C.

Pectin-destroying enzymes Added to ingredients high in pectin — apples, pears, plums — before fermentation. Pectin-destroying enzymes help prevent cloudiness in the fermented wine.

Potassium phosphate Assists rapid reproduction of yeast and quick fermentation of the wine.

Potassium sorbate Inhibits wine yeast from further activity in fermented wine ready for bulk storage to clear and mature, or bottling. Prevents 'popping' corks. Not for use in wines you want to make sparkle (see pages 68–69).

Precipitated chalk (calcium carbonate) Used to reduce acidity in fermenting wines or wine ready for bottling.

Rohament P (pectin glycoside) Mixed with cold water, extracts flavour and colour from natural ingredients prior to fermentation.

Sodium metabisulphite Sterilizing agent; kills and inhibits bacteria; prevents over-oxidation of wine by absorbing excess air introduced to the wine during syphoning or pouring (racking).

Succinic acid When added to a fermented wine, develops the wine's bouquet during storage.

Tannin Increases the wine's 'bite'; guards against over-oxidation; inhibits development of bacteria; assists clearing and maturation and improves keeping qualities.

Tartaric acid In its natural form found mainly in grapes. See 'Acid blends'.

Good health guide to natural ingredients

Natural wines, enjoyed in moderation, are good for our health and general well-being. Listed below is a selection of natural ingredients popular with country winemakers, together with some of the health-bestowing and healing properties credited to the ingredients through decades and often centuries of folk medicine.

These notes are included for your interest only: *no claims* are made for the healing value of any natural wines.

Agrimony Tonic and diuretic. Soothes sore throats.

Apple Rich in vitamins A, B, C and minerals: calcium, iron, phosphorous, potassium. Tonic. Improves complexion.

Apricot Contains vitamins A, B and C. High iron content – valuable in treatment of anaemia and asthma.

Banana High in vitamins A, B, C and minerals: calcium, iron, phosphorous and potassium. Supplies energy.

Barley Rich in vitamin B. Highly nutritious, body-building food. Easily digested by invalids. Can prevent asthma attacks.

Beetroot Good source of vitamins A, B and C; plus protein, calcium, iron and phosphorous. Strengthens blood and body's resistance to infection.

Bilberry Eases stomach upsets and reduces accumulation of fluid in body tissue.

Blackberry Contains vitamins A, B and C. Tonic and blood purifier.

Blackcurrant Tonic, natural antiseptic and blood purifier. Helps prevent colds and influenza; cures sore throats.

Carrot Contains wealth of vitamins: A, B, C, D, E and minerals. Prevents colds; improves complexion; general tonic and long credited with power to improve eyesight.

Celery Folk cure for anaemia, arthritis, asthma and rheumatism.

Cherry Used to treat anaemia, catarrh and rheumatism.

Coltsfoot High vitamin C content. Traditional cough cure.

Dandelion Tonic and mild laxative.

Elderberry Cold cure. Effective in treatment of sore throats and constipation.

Elderflower Eases stomach upsets and aids restful sleep.

Fig Extremely nutritious. Helps relieve asthma, coughs and bronchitis. Also mild laxative.

Root ginger Stimulant and expectorant.

Gooseberry Improves complexion; relieves catarrh and constipation.

Grape Contains vitamins A, B, C and minerals: calcium, iron and phosphorous. Source of 'instant' energy; nutritious, cleansing and vitalizing.

Grapefruit High in vitamins B and C. Assists digestion and improves complexion.

Hawthorn blossom Heart tonic. Improves circulation.

Honey Supplies vitamins B and C, plus many minerals. Easily digested high energy food. Beneficial in treatment of arthritis and rheumatism.

Hop Natural antiseptic. Purifies blood and encourages restful sleep.

Lemon Rich in vitamins B and C. Tonic. Natural antiseptic; blood purifier and cold cure.

Loganberry General tonic. Improves complexion; relieves constipation.

Nettle Nutritious tonic. High vitamin C and iron content. Strengthens blood, combats colds, arthritis and rheumatism.

Oak leaf Used in treatment of anaemia.

Orange High in vitamins A, B, C; calcium, iron, phosphorous and potassium. Effective in treatment of asthma, arthritis and rheumatism.

Parsley Rich in vitamins and minerals. Valuable in treatment of anaemia, arthritis and rheumatism.

Parsnip High in vitamin B. Remedy for insomnia and diarrhoea.

Passionfruit Relaxes nervous tension; assists restful sleep.
Pea pod Nourishing; strengthens blood.
Peach Improves complexion; relieves constipation.
Pear Eases catarrh; improves complexion.
Peppermint Tonic. Relieves indigestion. Effective cold cure.
Pineapple High in vitamins A, B, C; calcium, iron, phosphorous and potassium. Aids digestion. Beneficial in treatment of arthritis, catarrh and constipation.
Plum Assists digestion and improves complexion.
Potato Rich in vitamins A, B, C and minerals. High energy source. Helps in treatment of diarrhoea.
Prune Dried plum, see 'Plum'.
Raisin Dried black grape, see 'Grape'.
Raspberry Reduces anxiety; relaxes body.
Rhubarb (stalks only) Rich in vitamin C. Mild laxative. Cleanses the body and sharpens jaded appetite.
Rosehip Extremely high in vitamin C. Effective cold cure. Also eases sore throats and coughs.
Rose petal Used in treatment of arthritis.
Sloe High in vitamin C. Cold cure. Diuretic and mild laxative.
Strawberry Purifies blood and improves complexion.
Sultana Dried white grape, see 'Grape'.
Turnip Rich in vitamins B and C. Relieves nervous tension; aids sleep.
Walnut leaf Beneficial in cases of anaemia.
Wheat High in vitamin B. Assists in treatment of arthritis.

Honey

Honey, rich in B and C vitamins, natural enzymes and important minerals, has been highly valued for its precious medicinal and health-promoting qualities since ancient times.

Honey is of course made by bees from the nectar of flowers. It is a liquid food supplying the wealth of vitamins and healing properties credited to flowers visited by the bees.

The high natural sugar (fructose and glucose) content of pure honey is easily assimilated by the body and quickly turned into energy. Unlike processed sugar (sucrose) natural honey sugar (fructose and glucose) does not cause a craving for sweetness and is not habit-forming.

Pure honey has a long association with love and romance: honeyed wine was traditionally enjoyed by newlyweds for one lunar month while on 'honeymoon' to guarantee lively love-making and fertility.

Some modern research suggests honey rejuvenates and prolongs life; strengthens blood and circulation; improves the functioning of heart muscles and is beneficial in the treatment of anaemia, arthritis and rheumatism.

One pound (454 g) of liquid or pure set honey can replace 14 oz (397 g) of processed household sugar (sucrose) in any wine recipe. Honey greatly increases natural wine's full flavour, bouquet (aroma) and nutritional value.

There are many different types of pure honey; each enhances your wine's rich taste in a unique and delicious way. Among favourite honeys are: acacia blossom, clover, heather (for strongly flavoured meads), lime blossom, mixed blossom and orange blossom.

The one exception is eucalyptus blossom honey, which is overpowering in most wines and not to everyone's taste. Only use eucalyptus honey if you relish the flavour of eucalyptus!

Honey is a worthwhile addition to all your wines. Just a few grams of pure honey make a noticeable improvement to the grandest recipes.

Honey wine pick-me-up

An effective pick-me-up and cold cure can be made as follows:
To serve one
Wine (of your choice) – ¾ filled wine glass
Pure lemon juice – 3 teaspoons (15 ml)
Pure honey – 2 level (10 ml) teaspoons
Whole cloves – 2

Heat wine to simmering in small saucepan. Add lemon juice, honey and cloves; stir. Remove from heat, cover and allow to cool. Then re-heat, strain into a warmed glass or cup and drink while hot. For best results take before going to bed at night.

Chemical-free winemaking

Excellent wines have been made from natural ingredients for hundreds of years, without the need for chemical additives. The Romans were renowned for their superior quality wines, made from grapes and 'country' wines made from healing herbs. The Romans did not use packets of enzymes, nutrients and acids.

Your choice

Chemicals for winemaking can be helpful and beneficial, and may prevent the odd disaster (see pages 36–37) but it is wrong to think all chemicals are vital or irreplaceable. Chemicals are usually mass-marketed laboratory copies of elements freely available in natural ingredients. By careful blending of natural ingredients you can produce a mix that includes all necessary 'chemicals' in their natural form.

Winemaking recipes, similar to those in this log, which list pure honey, pure grape juice, raisins (dried black grapes) or sultanas (dried white grapes), lemons and/or oranges, and tea (tannin), contain all necessary acids, enzymes, minerals, nutrients and vitamins to ensure trouble-free, speedy and complete fermentation of delicious natural wine.

A case for chemicals

Harmful bacteria on winemaking equipment may infect and spoil your wine, unless you sterilize the equipment (see page 8). Chemical sterilants are 100 per cent effective and important to natural winemaking without risk. However, all traces of the sterilizing chemical *must be rinsed away* with water prior to use – no chemical must enter your wine.

Shopping

If you want to make nourishing natural wines, totally free of chemicals, then *read labels* when shopping. Check the contents list on labels before buying packaged 'natural' ingredients and reject those itemizing chemical additives.

Pure juices

Pure fruit and grape juices, ideal for winemaking, are available from supermarkets and health food stockists. Concentrated winemaking grape juices frequently contain chemical additives. Pure malt extract syrup, suitable for brewing beer and barley wine, is sold by homebrew and health food stockists.

Pure yeast

Pure wine and beer yeasts are available from your homebrew stockist. They are marketed as a living culture in small phials, and as dried granules in packets or tubs. Follow the directions for use that come with pure wine yeast or beer yeast. Some dried wine yeast compounds contain chemical additives.

Winemaking calendar

Here's a month-by-month guide to keep your demijohns filled and busy, bubbling with health-giving natural wine goodness, throughout the year.

JANUARY

Banana Barley Beetroot Blackcurrant juice (pure) Carrot Celery Dried fig Root ginger Orange Parsnip Potato Rice and raisin Turnip Wheat

FEBRUARY

Apple juice (pure) Banana Beetroot Carrot Celery Dried fig Grape juice Melomel (see page 71) Orange Parsnip Potato Tea and prune Turnip Wheat

MARCH

Banana Barley Carrot Coltsfoot Dandelion Grape juice Metheglin (see page 72) Orange Parsnip Passionfruit juice (pure) Potato Turnip

APRIL

Apple and blackcurrant juice (pure) Banana Carrot Coltsfoot Dandelion Gorse flower Grape juice Honey mead Oak leaf Orange Pineapple Rhubarb (stalks only) Turnip

MAY

Banana Dandelion Elderflower Gorse flower Grapefruit juice (pure) Hawthorn blossom Honey mead Nettle Oak leaf Orange Rhubarb (stalks only) Walnut leaf

JUNE

Apricot Beetroot Cherry Elderflower Gooseberry Gorse flower Hawthorn blossom Hop Nettle Oak leaf Orange Parsley Pea pod Peach Peppermint Plum Raspberry Rhubarb (stalks only) Rose petal Strawberry

JULY   Agrimony Apricot Blackcurrant Cherry Dandelion Gooseberry Gorse flower Hop Loganberry Melomel (see page 71) Parsley Pea pod Peppermint Raspberry Rhubarb (stalks only) Rose petal Strawberry

AUGUST   Agrimony Apricot Blackcurrant Carrot Cherry Dandelion Gooseberry Hop Loganberry Marrow Pea pod Peach Peppermint Plum Raspberry Rose petal Strawberry

SEPTEMBER   Apple Apricot Beetroot Bilberry Blackberry Blackcurrant Carrot Celery Damson Dandelion Elderberry Hop Marrow Morello cherry Parsnip Pea pod Peach Pear Pineapple Plum Potato Rosehip Sloe

OCTOBER   Apple Blackberry Carrot Celery Elderberry Grape juice Marrow Metheglin (see page 72) Orange Parsnip Peach Pear Pineapple Plum Potato Rosehip Sloe Turnip

NOVEMBER   Apple Banana Carrot Celery Elderberry Root ginger Grape juice Honey mead Orange Parsnip Pear Pineapple Potato Rosehip Sloe Tea and sultana Turnip

DECEMBER   Apple Banana Barley Beetroot Carrot Celery Dried fig Root ginger Grape juice Honey mead Orange juice (pure) Parsnip Pear Pineapple juice (pure) Potato Wheat

The hydrometer

Winemakers can use a hydrometer to measure the quantity of natural sugar (fructose and glucose) and/or processed household sugar (sucrose) in liquid about to be fermented into wine, and the amount of sugar (if any) left in wine after it has finished fermenting.

Regular readings taken with a hydrometer also indicate how quickly sugar is being converted to alcohol in a fermenting wine.

Specific gravity

Winemakers' hydrometers, clearly marked with a scale of numbers, are adjusted to float in water at 1.000 kg per litre. Any sugar present in the liquid raises the height at which the hydrometer floats. The more sugar present in the liquid, the higher the figure shown at the point where the base of the curved surface of liquid (the meniscus) meets the hydrometer's number scale. This figure is called the specific gravity.

By finding the appropriate figure in a set of hydrometer tables, you can predict the approximate level of alcohol that should be produced by the wine yeast's fermentation of sugar in the liquid. Because alcohol is lighter than water, a wine with all sugar converted to alcohol may show a hydrometer reading of less than 1.000; sometimes as low as 0.990.

A winemaker's *hydrometer trial jar* is useful for pouring samples of liquid to float the hydrometer, but any suitably deep, sterilized and rinsed jar or container can be used. The hydrometer does have limitations:

(a) Sugar present in many natural ingredients, especially whole fresh or dried fruit, does not immediately 'show up' on the first or subsequent hydrometer readings.

(b) Minute and often unfermentable 'solids' that form the body or texture of a full or heavy-bodied wine may buoy-up the floating hydrometer slightly above the 1.000 mark, even when all sugar has been converted to alcohol.

The hydrometer does not tell you when the wine has finished fermenting. You must rely on your own judgment (see recipes).

Many winemakers' hydrometers come complete with tables and full instructions, but here is an abbreviated and simplified table for your convenience.

Specific gravity	Sugar in gallons (4½ litres)	% Potential alcohol
1.020	7 oz (198 g)	2.5
1.040	1 lb (454 g)	5.5
1.060	1 lb 9 oz (709 g)	8
1.080	2 lb (907 g)	11
1.100	2½ lb (1.13 kg)	13.5
1.120	3 lb (1.36 kg)	16.5

A fermented dry (non-sweet) wine shows a final specific gravity reading of around 0.995; a medium wine about 1.005; sweet wine 1.010 and very sweet 1.020. Full-flavoured wines, strong in alcohol and rich in body, are frequently palatable with a final specific gravity as high as 1.030.

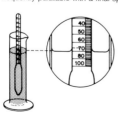

The reading is taken by eye at the level of the surface of the liquid

Here the correct reading is 70, and NOT 66

Name of wine:	Main ingredients:	Honey used:	Remarks:
Date yeast added:		Sugar:	
Date wine stored:			
Date clear:	Chemicals:	Final colour:	Date first bottle opened:
Date bottled:			Bouquet (aroma):
			Flavour:
			Alcohol (light/med/strong):

25

Name of wine:	Main ingredients:	Honey used:	Remarks:
Date yeast added:		Sugar:	
Date wine stored:			
Date clear:	Chemicals:	Final colour:	Date first bottle opened:
			Bouquet (aroma):
Date bottled:			Flavour:
			Alcohol (light/med/strong):

Name of wine:	Main ingredients:	Honey used:	Remarks:
Date yeast added:		Sugar:	
Date wine stored:			Date first bottle opened:
Date clear:	Chemicals:	Final colour:	Bouquet (aroma):
Date bottled:			Flavour:
			Alcohol (light/med/strong):

27

Name of wine:	Main ingredients:	Honey used:	Remarks:
Date yeast added:		Sugar:	
Date wine stored:			Date first bottle opened:
Date clear:	Chemicals:	Final colour:	Bouquet (aroma):
Date bottled:			Flavour:
			Alcohol (light/med/strong):

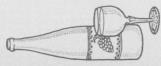

28

Name of wine:	Main ingredients:	Honey used:	Remarks:
Date yeast added:		Sugar:	
Date wine stored:			
			Date first bottle opened:
Date clear:	Chemicals:	Final colour:	Bouquet (aroma):
			Flavour:
Date bottled:			Alcohol (light/med/strong):

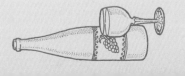

Name of wine:	Main ingredients:	Honey used:	Remarks:
Date yeast added:		Sugar:	
Date wine stored:			Date first bottle opened:
Date clear:	Chemicals:	Final colour:	Bouquet (aroma):
Date bottled:			Flavour:
			Alcohol (light/med/strong):

Name of wine:	Main ingredients:	Honey used:	Remarks:
Date yeast added:		Sugar:	
Date wine stored:			Date first bottle opened:
Date clear:	Chemicals:	Final colour:	Bouquet (aroma):
Date bottled:			Flavour:
			Alcohol (light/med/strong):

Name of wine:	Main ingredients:	Honey used:	Remarks:
Date yeast added:		Sugar:	
Date wine stored:			Date first bottle opened:
Date clear:	Chemicals:	Final colour:	Bouquet (aroma):
Date bottled:			Flavour:
			Alcohol (light/med/strong):

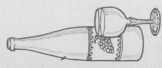

Glossary for winemakers

Winemakers' special words can be difficult to understand, particularly for those new to winemaking. This list offers instant understanding of mysterious 'wine-words', enabling you to follow expert chat and sound an authority when speaking to friends!

Acetification Wine turning 'sour' as a result of alcohol being converted to acetic acid by acetifying bacteria. Wine vinegar is the end result of this process, caused by:

(a) failure to sterilize equipment

(b) infection of uncovered fermenting wine by the fruit fly (*Drosophila melanogaster*)

(c) over-exposure of fermenting or stored wine to air.

Acidity The 'tart' taste of natural fruit acids in wine (see page 4). Correctly balanced, these acids bless wine with its mouth-watering appeal. In excess, the acidic 'tartness' may be unacceptably bitter. To remedy add honey to sweeten (see page 37).

Aerobic fermentation The action of wine yeast fermenting wine during the first stage of wine production (before an air lock is fitted).

Anaerobic fermentation The action of yeast fermenting wine in the absence of air (after the fermentation vessel has been filled and air lock fitted).

Astringent Sharp, dry (non-sweet) taste of wine due to excess tannin. For remedy, see page 37.

Autolysis Self destruction of wine yeast cells, notably after the yeast's maximum alcohol tolerance has been achieved by the fermenting wine (round 14% to 18% alcohol by volume). The dead yeast settles and steadily forms a firm sediment.

Binning Bulk storing bottles of wine ready for consumption. Special bins, racks or adequately supported piles of bottles, successfully 'bin' wine.

Malo-lactic fermentation Secondary fermentation of malic acid in bottled wine, giving the wine a pleasant sparkle, leading to the occasional blown cork! The malo-lactic fermentation is common in apple wine. To prevent popping corks, use *potassium sorbate*.

Fining Attempting to clear a cloudy or hazy wine by adding a chemical compound or natural ingredients (see page 36) to the maturing wine before bottling.

Laying down Traditionally, storing recently filled bottles of wine, 'laying down' until the wine has fully matured and is ready for 'binning' (see above) and drinking.

Maderization Madeira-like taste of wine which has been exposed to high temperatures for long periods.

Must Description of prepared solid and/or liquid ingredients prior to and during fermentation. When fermentation has ceased the 'must' has technically become wine.

Taint A distinctly unpleasant flavour in the matured wine, probably due to infection or spoilage during fermentation.

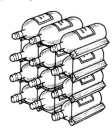

Caribbean sunset

Taste the tang of exotic Caribbean fruit freshness in this pure juice wine. An apéritif or after dinner drink. About 10.5% alcohol by volume.

To make 1 gallon (4½ litres)

Pure pineapple juice – 1 pint (568 ml)
Pure orange juice – ½ pint (284 ml)
Pure white grape juice – 1¾ pints (1 litre) or concentrated white winemaking grape juice – ½ pint (284 ml)
Pure lime blossom honey – 1 lb (454 g)
Sultanas – 8 oz (227 g)
Strong brewed tea – ½ teacup or winemaking grape tannin – 15 drops
Wine yeast – amount recommended by manufacturer
Water – to 1 gallon (4½ litres)

Sterilize and rinse equipment (see page 8). Dissolve honey in 1 pint (568 ml) of simmering water. Cover and leave to cool. Brew tea, allow to cool. Rinse sultanas in colander under running warm water. Chop or mince sultanas. Pour cool dissolved honey, tea or grape tannin, pineapple, orange and grape juice into plastic (food grade) bucket. Add sultanas, wine yeast and cold water to raise the total quantity of liquid to about 7 pints (4 litres); cover. Keep in a warm place, about 18%C (64°F) for seven days. Stir twice daily.

After seven days Pour or scoop the fermenting wine from its sediment and strain into a 1 gallon (4½ litre) demijohn; top up to the neck with cold water. Discard strained solids. Fit bung and air lock filled with water or sulphite solution (see page 7). Leave in the warm until fermentation is complete. Fermentation has finished when bubbles have ceased passing through the liquid in the air lock; when your wine tastes dry (non-sweet), is not fizzy on your tongue, and is beginning to fall clear from the surface downwards. When satisfied fermentation has ended, rack wine (see page 40) from its sediment into a sterilized, rinsed 1 gallon (4½ litre) vessel and top up to the neck with cold water. Add a crushed Campden tablet (optional); fit a cork or rubber bung. Store somewhere cool to clear and mature before bottling (see page 49).

Your Caribbean sunset should be clear and ready to bottle about four months after being stored to mature. Ready to drink two months after being bottled.

Rose petal rosé

Glowing rosé wine. Serve cool. About 10.5% alcohol by volume.

To make 1 gallon (4½ litres)

Fresh rose petals, mixed – 3½ pints (2 litres) or
dried rose petals – 3 oz (85g)
Pure red grape juice – 3½ pints (2 litres) or
concentrated red winemaking grape juice – 1 pint
(568 ml)
Granulated sugar (optional, see below) – 1¼ lb
(567 g)
Lemons – 2
Strong brewed tea – ½ teacup or
winemaking grape tannin – 15 drops
Wine yeast – amount recommended by manufacturer
Water – to 1 gallon (4½ litres)

Sugar free! To replace all granulated sugar (sucrose) with natural sugar (fructose and glucose) contained in natural ingredients (see page 5) miss out granulated sugar. Instead, add 1 lb (454 g) pure orange blossom honey, and 13 oz (369 g) sultanas.

Sterilize and rinse equipment (see page 8). Dissolve granulated sugar (if used) and/or honey in 2 pints (1¼ litres) simmering water. Cover and leave to cool. Brew tea, allow to cool. Rinse fresh rose petals in cold water; rinse sultanas (if used) in a colander under running warm water. Chop or mince sultanas. Extract juice from lemons. Pour cool dissolved sugar and/or honey, tea or grape tannin, grape juice, and lemon juice into plastic (food grade) bucket. Add sultanas (if used) wine yeast and cold water to raise total liquid to about 7 pints (4 litres); cover. Keep in warm for seven days. Stir twice daily.
After seven days Strain fermenting wine into 1 gallon (4½ litre), demijohn; top up to neck with cold water. Discard solids. Fit bung and air lock filled with water, or sulphite solution (see page 7). Leave in warm until fermentation is complete. Fermentation has finished when bubbles have ceased passing through liquid in the air lock; when your wine tastes dry (non-sweet), is not fizzy on your tongue, and is beginning to fall clear from the surface downwards. When satisfied fermentation has ceased, rack wine (see page 40) from its sediment into sterilized, rinsed 1 gallon (4½ litre) vessel; top up to neck with cold water. Add crushed Campden tablet (optional); fit cork or rubber bung. Store somewhere cool.

Your rose petal rosé should be clear and ready to bottle (see page 40) about three months after being stored to mature. Ready to drink two months after being bottled.

Answers to winemakers' problems

To avoid most problems, keep your equipment clean; sterilize before use (see page 8) and follow recipes carefully. Occasionally, however, your patience and knowledge of winemaking will be tested by unexpected and unwelcome developments in your fermenting or stored wine.

Bouquet (aroma), lack of

A wine's bouquet evolves as natural acids in ingredients blend and interact. The bouquet achieves a good standard about six months after the matured wine has been bottled.

To ensure your wine develops a full and appealing bouquet, add some grape juice, pure honey and pure lemon or orange juice to your natural ingredients before fermenting.

For prize-winning wines include a pinch of fresh or dried elderflowers or rose petals.

Winemaker's *succinic acid* may also be added, as directed by the manufacturer, after wine has finished fermenting, to assist progress of the bouquet.

Cloudiness

Cloudy wines usually clear if stored in a cool place to mature. However, you can speed the process by testing for the cause of cloudiness and taking appropriate action.

Pectin haze Common in wines where natural ingredients have been boiled or scalded with hot water. Cold water fermentation largely avoids pectin hazes.

Test for the presence of pectin with a special winemaker's testing kit, or pour 15 ml methylated spirit into a small jar and add a teaspoon (5 ml) of the cloudy wine. Cover and leave for two hours. If clots have appeared in the mixture, the haze is due to pectin.

Remedy Mix the quantity directed by the manufacturer of winemaker's pectin destroying enzyme into a cupful of cloudy wine; pour back into vessel of hazy wine and leave in cool for seven to fourteen days to clear.

Starch haze Sometimes found in wines made from grain or vegetables. Boiling or scalding ingredients aggravates this problem.

Test for starch with a winemaker's testing kit, or pour 15 ml of cloudy wine into a small jar and add a few drops of iodine. If starch is present the wine turns purple.

Remedy Mix the quantity directed by the manufacturer of winemaker's fungal amylase into a cupful of the hazy wine; pour back into vessel of hazy wine and leave in cool for seven to fourteen days to clear.

Clearing cloudy wines the natural way

To clear 1 gallon (4½ litres) of cloudy wine naturally, try this powerful preparation:

Fresh, skimmed milk – 2 tablespoons
Egg white – 1
Strong, brewed tea – 2 tablespoons

Measure the skimmed milk, egg white and brewed tea into a clean cup; add some cloudy wine and mix thoroughly. Then pour back into vessel of hazy wine and leave in cool for seven to fourteen days to clear.

Tip

Use two egg whites in the above preparation to clear seemingly 'unconquerable' cloudy wine.

Dryness (non-sweetness)

Wine too dry for your taste may be sweetened before serving, by stirring caster sugar or pure honey into the dry wine (see page 53).

Infection – general

In the unlikely event of your wine being infected by bacteria (off-flavours, surface film developing etc), one or two crushed Campden tablets added to 1 gallon (4½ litres) of infected wine immediately kills and/or inhibits growth of bacteria. Raising the natural acid level of wine by adding juice from two lemons (citric acid) kills bacteria and/or effectively prevents further bacterial activity; as does heating the wine briefly to simmering point in a large saucepan or saucepans. Remove by 'blotting' with clean white blotting paper.

Where Campden tablets or heating methods are used with fermenting wine, the wine yeast may be destroyed. To complete fermentation, add fresh wine yeast twenty-four hours after treating the wine.

Oiliness

Tiny patches of oil on the surface of fermented wine can occur when dried fruit is not rinsed under running warm water before being prepared for fermentation. Remove by 'blotting' with clean white blotting paper.

Sulphur smell

Your fermented wine is ready for storing prior to bottling, but has the unpleasant and unmistakeable smell of sulphite solution (see page 8) or Campden tablets.

You did not rinse away all traces of sterilizing solution from equipment before beginning fermentation, or you have put too many crushed Campden tablets in the wine. Commercial wines contain the equivalent of up to six Campden tablets per gallon (4½ litres) of wine, but a total of three crushed Campden tablets per gallon should be adequate for our wines.

Remedy Aerate the wine by pouring from one container to another two or three times before sealing and leaving to adjust and mature.

Sweetness

Your fermented wine is ready to store and mature before bottling, but tastes too sweet for your palate.

Remedy Either mix and blend with a dry (non-sweet) wine of similar colour and flavour, or re-start the fermentation by adding Champagne yeast to ferment the sweet wine to dryness.

N.B. Champagne yeast is unlikely to ferment wine that has formed a very high alcohol content (above 14% alcohol by volume). Blend strong, sweet wine with a dry wine (see above).

Vinegar smell

The acetobacter group of bacteria have infected your wine, which has probably been in contact with unsterilized equipment or left uncovered and exposed to the air. In any event, your only course of action must be to convert fully your infected wine to wine vinegar (see page 81).

Sake

Powerful rice wine. Serve at room temperature, or heated in warmed glasses. About 12.5% alcohol by volume.

To make 1 gallon (4½ litres)

Brown rice – 2¼ lb (1 kg)
Sultanas – 8 oz (227 g)
Demerara sugar (optional, see below) – 2¼ lb (1 kg)
Lemons – 3
Strong brewed tea – ½ teacup *or* winemaking grape tannin – 15 drops
Wine yeast – amount recommended by manufacturer
Water – to 1 gallon (4½ litres)

Sugar free! To replace all demerara sugar (sucrose) with natural sugar (fructose and glucose) contained in natural ingredients (see page 5) miss out demerara sugar; instead add 1 lb (454 g) pure acacia blossom honey, 3½ pints (2 litres) pure white grape juice *or* 1 pint (568 ml) concentrated white winemaking grape juice and 8 oz (227 g) extra sultanas.

Sterilize and rinse equipment (see page 8). Dissolve demerara sugar (if any) and/or honey in 2 pints (1¼ litres) simmering water. Cover; leave to cool. Brew tea, allow to cool. Rinse rice and sultanas separately in colander under running warm water. Chop or mince sultanas. Extract juice from lemons. Pour cool dissolved sugar and/or honey, tea or grape tannin, grape juice (if any) and lemon juice into plastic (food grade) bucket. Add sultanas and rice, wine yeast and cold water to raise total liquid to about 7 pints (4 litres); cover. Keep in warm place for seven days. Stir twice daily.

After seven days Strain fermenting sake into 1 gallon (4½ litre) demijohn; top up to neck with cold water. Discard solids. Fit bung and air lock filled with water, or sulphite solution (see page 7). Leave in warm until fermentation is complete. Fermentation has finished when bubbles have ceased passing through liquid in the air lock; when your sake tastes dry (non-sweet), is not fizzy on your tongue, and is beginning to fall clear from the surface downwards. When satisfied fermentation has ceased, rack sake (see page 40) from its sediment into sterilized, rinsed 1 gallon (4½ litre) vessel; top up to neck with cold water. Add crushed Campden tablet (optional); fit cork or rubber bung. Store somewhere cool.

Your sake should be clear and ready to bottle (see page 40) about four months after being stored to mature. Ready to drink two months after being bottled.

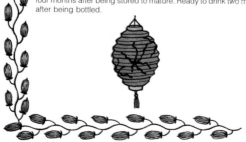

Dandelion delight

Smooth, golden wine. Excellent chilled and served as a white table wine or social wine. About 10.5% alcohol by volume.

To make 1 gallon (4½ litres)

Fresh dandelion heads – 3½ pints (2 litres) or
dried dandelion heads – 3 oz (85 g)
Pure mixed blossom honey – 8 oz (227 g)
Sultanas – 8 oz (227 g)
Granulated sugar (optional, see below) – 1¼ lb (567 g)
Oranges – 3, medium sized
Strong brewed tea – ½ teacup or winemaking grape tannin – 15 drops
Wine yeast – amount recommended by manufacturer
Water – to 1 gallon (4½ litres)

Sugar free! To replace all granulated sugar (sucrose) with natural sugar (fructose and glucose) contained in natural ingredients (see page 5) miss out granulated sugar; instead *add* 3½ pints (2 litres) pure white grape juice *or* 1 pint (568 ml) concentrated white winemaking grape juice and 8 oz (227 g) extra sultanas.

Sterilize and rinse equipment (see page 8). Dissolve granulated sugar (if used) and/or honey in 2 pints (1¼ litres) simmering water. Cover; leave to cool. Brew tea, allow to cool. Rinse fresh dandelion heads in cold water and rinse sultanas in colander under running warm water. Chop or mince sultanas. Extract juice from oranges. Pour cool dissolved sugar and/or honey, tea or grape tannin, grape juice (if used) and orange juice into plastic (food grade) bucket. Add sultanas, wine yeast and cold water to raise total liquid to about 7 pints (4 litres); cover. Keep in warm for seven days. Stir twice daily.
After seven days Strain fermenting wine into 1 gallon (4½ litre) demijohn; top up to neck with cold water. Discard solids. Fit bung and air lock filled with water, or sulphite solution (see page 7). Leave in warm until fermentation is complete. Fermentation has finished when bubbles have ceased passing through liquid in the air lock; when your wine tastes dry (non-sweet); is not fizzy on your tongue, and is beginning to fall clear from the surface downwards. When satisfied fermentation has ceased, rack wine (see page 40) from its sediment into sterilized, rinsed 1 gallon (4½ litre) vessel; top up to neck with cold water. Add crushed Campden tablet (optional); fit cork or rubber bung. Store somewhere cool.

Your dandelion delight should be clear and ready to bottle (see page 40) about five months after being stored to mature. Ready to drink two months after being bottled.

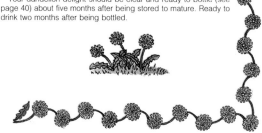

Racking and bottling

Fermenting or fermented wine is 'racked' whenever it is poured, scooped or syphoned from its sediment into another container, or finally bottled.

Whole and liquid ingredients, fermenting together in a bucket, are most easily racked and strained (see recipes) into a demijohn with the aid of a jug, winemaker's fine mesh straining bag or plastic strainer, and a plastic funnel. The fermenting wine is simply scooped from the bucket and strained into your demijohn.

When wine has finished fermenting (see recipes) it should again be racked from its sediment into a clean, sterilized and rinsed demijohn and stored to clear and mature before being bottled. If the only such vessel you have is the one you are using, rack the wine into a sterilized, rinsed (food grade) bucket and cover. Clean, sterilize and rinse the demijohn then pour the wine from your bucket back into the vessel and fit a sterilized, rinsed cork or rubber bung.

Bottles

After your wine has cleared and been stored for the minimum period recommended in the recipe, rack from sediment into bottles. One gallon (4½ litres) of wine fills six or six and a half standard size wine bottles, depending on the amount of sediment later discarded. Clean, sterilize and rinse bottles.

Corks and stoppers

Straight-sided corks require a special winemaker's corking tool to thrust them down inside the bottle neck, and should be softened before use by soaking for twenty-four hours in a sealed jar of sulphite solution (see page 8). Cork or plastic stoppers don't need 'softening' or a corking tool; stoppers can be pushed into place. Sterilize cork stoppers by soaking in a sealed jar filled with sulphite solution for thirty minutes; briefly submerge plastic stoppers. *Rinse all corks or stoppers with water before use.*

Syphon

To rack wine into bottles without disturbing sediment, use a sterilized, rinsed 4 ft (1.2 m) length of winemaker's plastic syphon tube. A small attachable on/off tap is helpful.

Method

Place the 1 gallon (4½ litre) vessel of wine on a strong, level surface higher than the bottles to be filled. Add one crushed Campden tablet (optional) to the wine. Lower the syphon tube into the wine until it rests slightly above the sediment at the bottom of the vessel. Put a plastic funnel into the neck of your first bottle. Turn on the tap and suck wine into the syphon tube; direct the flow of wine along the funnel into your bottle. Fill each bottle to within 2¼ inches (57 mm) of its mouth.

When bottling is complete, fit straight sided corks or stoppers. Then label and store (see page 49).

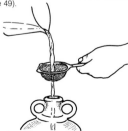

Name of wine:	Main ingredients:	Honey used:	Remarks:
Date yeast added:		Sugar:	
Date wine stored:			
			Date first bottle opened:
Date clear:	Chemicals:	Final colour:	Bouquet (aroma):
			Flavour:
Date bottled:			Alcohol (light/med/strong):

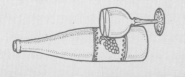

41

Name of wine:	Main ingredients:	Honey used:	Remarks:
Date yeast added:		Sugar:	
Date wine stored:			Date first bottle opened:
Date clear:	Chemicals:	Final colour:	Bouquet (aroma):
Date bottled:			Flavour:
			Alcohol (light/med/strong):

Name of wine:	Main ingredients:	Honey used:	Remarks:
Date yeast added:		Sugar:	
Date wine stored:			Date first bottle opened:
Date clear:	Chemicals:	Final colour:	Bouquet (aroma):
Date bottled:			Flavour:
			Alcohol (light/med/strong):

43

Name of wine:	Main ingredients:	Honey used:	Remarks:
Date yeast added:		Sugar:	
Date wine stored:			
Date clear:	Chemicals:	Final colour:	Date first bottle opened:
			Bouquet (aroma):
Date bottled:			Flavour:
			Alcohol (light/med/strong):

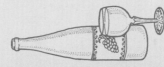

44

Name of wine:	Main ingredients:	Honey used:	Remarks:
Date yeast added:		Sugar:	
Date wine stored:			
Date clear:	Chemicals:	Final colour:	Date first bottle opened:
			Bouquet (aroma):
Date bottled:			Flavour:
			Alcohol (light/med/strong):

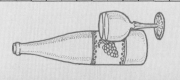

45

Name of wine:

Main ingredients:

Honey used:

Remarks:

Date yeast added:

Sugar:

Date wine stored:

Date clear:

Chemicals:

Final colour:

Date first bottle opened:

Bouquet (aroma):

Date bottled:

Flavour:

Alcohol (light/med/strong):

Name of wine:	Main ingredients:	Honey used:	Remarks:
Date yeast added:		Sugar:	
Date wine stored:			
			Date first bottle opened:
Date clear:	Chemicals:	Final colour:	Bouquet (aroma):
Date bottled:			Flavour:
			Alcohol (light/med/strong):

47

Name of wine:	Main ingredients:	Honey used:	Remarks:
Date yeast added:		Sugar:	
Date wine stored:			
Date clear:	Chemicals:	Final colour:	Date first bottle opened:
			Bouquet (aroma):
Date bottled:			Flavour:
			Alcohol (light/med/strong):

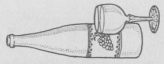

Labelling and storage

Clean the outside of your wine filled bottles with a soapy cloth. Rinse away traces of detergent; dry and polish with a towel. Then print or write neatly the name of your wine on an attractive label. You may include a personalized message if the bottle is intended as a gift. Always make a note on the label of the date the fermented wine was stored to clear and mature before being bottled (so you know how mature the wine is); also record the date of bottling in your log.

Glue the label about 1½ inches (38 mm) below the bottle's shoulder, and between the two seams along the bottle's sides. Smooth out wrinkles with a clean, dry cloth.

Push a coloured plastic or foil cap over the bottle top for that professional touch. Your bottled wine should delight the eye almost as much as the delicious contents appeal to the palate.

Storage

Store your wine somewhere cool, dry and out of direct sunlight. An even temperature of about 10°C (50°F) is ideal. A rack, bin, bottle carton or cardboard box may be used, and bins, cartons and boxes are easily stacked. Mark contents on the outside of boxes for immediate location of vintage years.

Wine should be left to condition in bottles for at least two months before being served. All wines improve rapidly for a minimum of six months after being bottled. Never hurry a good wine. The wait is always worthwhile. All the recipes in this log suggest when you can expect your wine to be matured.

Tip
Sunken corks

When an empty bottle is returned to you with the cork forced down inside the bottle; remove the cork by filling the bottle with cold water; manoeuvre a thin piece of looped wire underneath the floating cork, and firmly pull looped wire upwards. The cork will pop out and your bottle will be saved.

Elderberry wine

Rich red table wine. About 12.5% alcohol by volume.

N.B. Elderberries are high in natural tannin: no tea or grape tannin is necessary in this recipe.

To make 1 gallon (4½ litres)

Fresh elderberries—3¼ lb (1½ kg) *or* dried elderberries—12 oz (340 g)
Pure mixed blossom honey—8 oz (227 g)
Pure red grape juice—1¾ pints (1 litre) *or* concentrated red winemaking grape juice—½ pint (284 ml)
Raisins—8 oz (227 g)
Granulated sugar (optional, see below)—14 oz (397 g)
Lemons—2
Wine yeast—amount recommended by manufacturer
Water—to 1 gallon (4½ litres)

Sugar free! To replace all granulated sugar (sucrose) with natural sugar (fructose and glucose) contained in natural ingredients (see page 5) miss out granulated sugar; instead add extra 1¾ pints (1 litre) pure red grape juice *or* ½ pint (284 ml) concentrated red winemaking grape juice and 8 oz (227 g) extra pure mixed blossom honey.

Rinse *dried* elderberries (if used) in warm water; then soak for twenty-four hours in cold water before mashing in bucket. Sterilize and rinse equipment (see page 8). Dissolve granulated sugar (if used) and/or honey in 2 pints (1¼ litres) simmering water. Cover; leave to cool. Rinse fresh elderberries in cold water; place in plastic (food grade) bucket and mash. Cover bucket. Rinse raisins in colander under running warm water. Chop or mince raisins. Extract juice from lemons. Pour cool dissolved sugar and/or honey, grape juice and lemon juice into bucket. Add raisins, wine yeast and cold water to raise total liquid to about 7 pints (4 litres); cover. Keep in warm for seven days. Stir twice daily.

After seven days Strain fermenting wine into 1 gallon (4½ litre) demijohn; top up to neck with cold water. Discard solids. Fit bung and air lock filled with water, or sulphite solution (see page 7). Leave in warm until fermentation is complete. Fermentation has finished when bubbles have ceased passing through liquid in the air lock; when your wine tastes dry (non-sweet); is not fizzy on your tongue; and is beginning to fall clear from the surface downwards. When satisfied fermentation has ceased, rack wine (see page 40) from its sediment into sterilized, rinsed 1 gallon (4½ litre) vessel; top up to neck with cold water. Add crushed Campden tablet (optional); fit cork or rubber bung. Store somewhere cool.

Your elderberry wine should be clear and ready to bottle (see page 40) about seven months after being stored to mature. Ready to drink two months after being bottled.

Apple wine

Light white wine. About 10% alcohol by volume.

To make 1 gallon (4½ litres)

Apples, mixed – 2¼ lb (1 kg)
Pure apple juice – 1¾ pints (1 litre)
Pure acacia blossom honey – 12 oz (340 g)
Pure white grape juice – 1¾ pints (1 litre)
or
concentrated white winemaking grape juice – ½ pint (284 ml)
Sultanas – 10 oz (283 g)
Lemon – 1
Strong brewed tea – ½ teacup or winemaking grape tannin – 15 drops
Wine yeast – amount recommended by manufacturer
Water – to 1 gallon (4½ litres)

Sterilize and rinse equipment (see page 8). Dissolve honey in 1 pint (568 ml) of simmering water. Cover and leave to cool. Brew tea, allow to cool. Wash apples in warm water; cut out and discard diseased parts. Quarter *unpeeled* apples; remove and discard cores and pips. Slice apple quarters thinly. Place apple slices in plastic (food grade) bucket; cover. Rinse sultanas in colander under running warm water. Chop or mince sultanas. Extract juice from lemon; discard peel, pith and pips. Pour cool dissolved honey, tea or grape tannin, grape juice and lemon juice into bucket. Add sultanas, wine yeast and cold water to raise the total quantity of liquid to about 7 pints (4 litres); cover. Keep in a warm place, around 18°C (64° F) for seven days. Stir twice daily.

After seven days Pour or scoop the fermenting wine from its sediment and strain into a 1 gallon (4½ litre) demijohn; top up to the neck with cold water. Discard strained solids. Fit bung and air lock filled with water, or sulphite solution (see page 7). Leave in the warm until fermentation is complete. Fermentation has finished when bubbles have ceased passing through the liquid in the air lock; when your wine tastes dry (non-sweet); is not fizzy on your tongue, and is beginning to fall clear from the surface downwards. When satisfied fermentation has ended, rack wine (see page 40) from its sediment into a sterilized, rinsed 1 gallon (4½ litre) vessel and top up to the neck with cold water. Add a crushed Campden tablet (optional); fit a cork or rubber bung. Store somewhere cool to clear and mature before bottling (see page 49).

Your apple wine should be clear and ready to bottle about three months after being stored to mature. Ready to drink two months after being bottled.

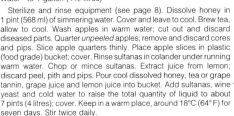

Choosing the right wine

Always have a bottle of both red and white wine ready to offer unexpected guests. Stand selected 'special reserve' bottles upright so sediment settles at the bottom of the bottle.

With the obvious exception of sparkling wine, all wines improve in quality if permitted to *breathe* air for at least two hours before being served. To admit air remove the cork, or decant your wine ready for serving by carefully pouring the wine into a decanter. Take care to leave any sediment at the bottle's base.

Cool rosé wines before serving; chill white wines and serve sparkling wines cold. Thirty to ninety minutes in the refrigerator is sufficient.

Red wines and liqueurs should be served at room temperature.

Tulip shaped clear glasses enhance the appearance and bouquet of all wines and may be used in place of the different styles of glass traditionally ascribed to various wine types.

To help choose suitable wines to accompany and complement meals, the division of commercial wines into red, rosé and white can be applied to home made natural wines, although shades of colour vary widely.

White table wines can include: Apple, Apricot, Coltsfoot, Dandelion, Elderflower, Gooseberry, White grape, Grapefruit, Hawthorn blossom, Parsley, Passionfruit juice, Pea pod, Peach, Pear, Pineapple, Rhubarb (stalks only).

Rosé wines can include: Blackcurrant, Black grape, Loganberry, Orange, Plum, Raspberry, Rosehip, Rose petal, Strawberry.

Red table wines can include: Beetroot, Bilberry, Blackberry, Cherry, Elderberry, Black grape, Sloe.

Wines drunk on their own

Full-bodied natural wines, strong in flavour and alcohol, are best served as after-dinner wines.

Among excellent appetite-sharpening apéritifs are light white table wines: Apple, Elderflower, Gooseberry, Grapefruit, Pear, Pineapple, Rose petal etc.

Wines to accompany food

Remember that curry and highly spiced food taste better with chilled lager and that vinegar on food spoils the flavour of wine.

Some foods are traditionally accompanied by a certain type of wine:

Hors d'oeuvres, fish, white meat, salads Any dry or medium white table wine.
Pasta Any dry white table wine.
Red meat, game Any red table wine.
Sweet foods Any sweet white table wine.

How to sweeten wine

Before serving, stir and dissolve pure honey or caster sugar in half a cupful of selected dry wine poured from the bottle or decanter. Adjust the amount of pure honey or caster sugar to suit your taste, or that of your guests. A half to one level tablespoon of either honey or sugar is normally adequate to sweeten one bottle of wine. Mix the sweetened wine with the dry wine by pouring back into your bottle or decanter. Wait a few minutes to permit the wine to settle, then serve.

Party success secrets for the home wine-maker

1 Allow ½ to ⅔ of a bottle of wine per person.
2 Fill glasses ⅔ full, never more. (A bottle of wine pours seven glasses.)

Wine and cheese parties

Serve white and rosé wines with mild cheeses and red wine with full-flavoured cheeses.

White and rosé wines Brie, Caerphilly, Cheshire, English Cheddar, Wensleydale etc.
Red wines Camembert, Double Gloucester, Gorgonzola, Leicester, Stilton.

Peach wine

Succulent light rosé table wine. About 9.5% alcohol by volume. Fruit wines may be made with either fresh, canned, or bottled fruit.

To make 1 gallon (4½ litres)

Fresh peaches – 2¼ lb (1 kg) *or*
canned peaches, including syrup – 1 lb (454 g)
Pure mixed blossom honey – 12 oz (340 g)
Pure red grape juice – 3½ pints (2 litres) *or*
concentrated red winemaking grape juice – 1 pint (568 ml)
Sultanas – 12 oz (340 g)
Oranges – 2, medium sized
Strong brewed tea – ½ teacup *or* winemaking grape tannin – 15 drops
Wine yeast – amount recommended by manufacturer
Water – to 1 gallon (4½ litres)

Sterilize and rinse equipment (see page 8). Add canned peach syrup (if used) to 1 pint (568 ml) of water and simmer. Dissolve honey in simmering water. Cover, leave to cool. Brew tea, allow to cool. Wash fresh peaches (if used) in cold water; cut out and discard diseased parts. Cut fresh peaches in half; remove and discard stones. Place fresh or canned peaches in plastic (food grade) bucket and mash. Cover bucket. Rinse sultanas in colander under running warm water. Chop or mince sultanas. Extract juice from oranges; discard peel, pith and pips. Pour cool dissolved honey and peach syrup (if used), tea or grape tannin, grape juice, and orange juice into bucket. Add sultanas, wine yeast and cold water to raise the total quantity of liquid to about 7 pints (4 litres); cover. Keep in a warm place, around 18°C (64°F) for seven days. Stir twice daily.

After seven days Pour or scoop the fermenting wine from its sediment and strain into a 1 gallon (4½ litre) demijohn; top up to the neck with cold water. Discard strained solids. Fit bung and air lock filled with water, or sulphite solution (see page 7). Leave in the warm until fermentation is complete. Fermentation has finished when bubbles have ceased passing through the liquid in the air lock; when your wine tastes dry (non-sweet); is not fizzy on your tongue, and is beginning to fall clear from the surface downwards. When satisfied fermentation has ended, rack wine (see page 40) from its sediment into a sterilized, rinsed 1 gallon (4½ litre) vessel and top up to the neck with cold water. Add a crushed Campden tablet (optional); fit a cork or rubber bung. Store somewhere cool to clear and mature before bottling (see page 49).

Your peach wine should be clear and ready to bottle about three months after being stored to mature. Ready to drink two months after being bottled.

Barley wine

Rich and nourishing beverage. About 12% alcohol by volume.

To make 1 gallon (4½ litres)
Pearl barley – 1 lb (454 g) or
flaked barley – 1 lb (454 g)
*Pure malt extract syrup – 2 lb (907 g)
Pure clover honey – 1 lb (454 g)
Potatoes – 1 lb (454 g)
Lemons – 3
Strong brewed tea – ½ teacup or
winemaking grape tannin – 15 drops
Wine yeast – amount recommended by
manufacturer
Water – to 1 gallon (4½ litres)

*1 lb (454 g) of pure malt extract syrup contains
about 12 oz (340 g) of natural malt sugar
(maltose).

Sterilize and rinse equipment (see page 8). Dissolve honey and pure malt extract in 3½ pints (2 litres) of simmering water. Cover and leave to cool. Brew tea, allow to cool. Peel potatoes, discard peel. Remove and discard any green parts. Chop potatoes. Rinse pearl barley (not flaked barley) in colander under running warm water. Extract juice from lemons; discard peel, pith and pips. Pour cool dissolved honey and malt, tea or grape tannin, and lemon juice into plastic (food grade) bucket. Add barley, potatoes, wine yeast and cold water to raise the total quantity of liquid to about 7 pints (4 litres); cover. Keep in a warm place, about 18°C (64°F) for seven days. Stir twice daily.

After seven days Pour or scoop the fermenting wine from its sediment and strain into a 1 gallon (4½ litre) demijohn; top up to the neck with cold water. Discard strained solids. Fit bung and air lock filled with water, or sulphite solution (see page 7). Leave in the warm until fermentation is complete. Fermentation has finished when bubbles have ceased passing through the liquid in the air lock; when your wine tastes dry (non-sweet); is not fizzy on your tongue, and is beginning to fall clear from the surface downwards. When satisfied fermentation has ended, rack wine (see page 40) from its sediment into a sterilized, rinsed 1 gallon (4½ litre) vessel and top up to the neck with cold water. Add a crushed Campden tablet (optional); fit a cork or rubber bung. Store somewhere cool to clear and mature before bottling (see page 49).

Your barley wine should be clear and ready to bottle about four months after being stored to mature. Ready to drink two months after being bottled.

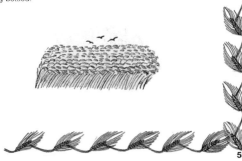

Fruit liqueurs

Luscious fruit liqueurs are easy to make. Any fresh fruit may be marinated in brandy, gin or vodka to quickly produce a cheering liqueur.

Six Star Advocaat

Tasty, extra-strong and creamy liqueur.

To make 1 wine bottle

Egg yolks – 6
Pure honey – 8 oz (227 g)
Brandy – 12 fl oz (341 ml)
Lemons – 2
Water, cold – 2 tablespoons

Extract juice from lemons. Discard pips, pith and peel. Pour lemon juice into mixing bowl. Add egg yolks, honey and cold water. Whisk ingredients in a bowl held over a saucepan of hot water until thick. Move thickened ingredients away from hot water; gradually whisk in brandy. Then place bowl back over saucepan of hot water and continue whisking until mixture is thick and creamy. Remove to somewhere safe; cover and allow to cool and settle. Then pour through funnel into a bottle, fasten cork or plastic stopper. Ready to drink in seven days.

Peach brandy

To make 1 wine bottle

Peaches, fresh – 1 lb (454 g)
Pure honey – 8 oz (227 g)
Brandy – 19 fl oz (540 ml)
Orange – 1

Wash peaches in cold water. Cut in half and remove stones. Slice peaches and place in large screw top jar. Extract juice from orange. Discard pips, pith and skin. Pour orange juice into jar. Add honey and brandy. Stir well. Fasten screw top and store somewhere dark. Stir daily for seven days, then leave for nine weeks.

After nine weeks strain into a bottle and fit cork or plastic stopper. Your peach brandy is now ready to drink. You can eat the preserved fruit.

Name of wine:	Main ingredients:	Honey used:	Remarks:
Date yeast added:		Sugar:	
Date wine stored:			
Date clear:	Chemicals:	Final colour:	Date first bottle opened:
			Bouquet (aroma):
Date bottled:			Flavour:
			Alcohol (light/med/strong):

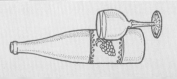

Name of wine:	Main ingredients:	Honey used:	Remarks:
Date yeast added:		Sugar:	
Date wine stored:			Date first bottle opened:
Date clear:	Chemicals:	Final colour:	Bouquet (aroma):
Date bottled:			Flavour:
			Alcohol (light/med/strong):

58

Name of wine:	Main ingredients:	Honey used:	Remarks:
		Sugar:	
Date yeast added:			
Date wine stored:			Date first bottle opened:
Date clear:	Chemicals:	Final colour:	Bouquet (aroma):
			Flavour:
Date bottled:			Alcohol (light/med/strong):

Name of wine:

Main ingredients:

Honey used:

Sugar:

Remarks:

Date yeast added:

Date wine stored:

Date clear:

Chemicals:

Final colour:

Date first bottle opened:

Bouquet (aroma):

Date bottled:

Flavour:

Alcohol (light/med/strong):

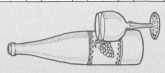

Name of wine:	Main ingredients:	Honey used:	Remarks:
Date yeast added:		Sugar:	
Date wine stored:			
Date clear:	Chemicals:	Final colour:	Date first bottle opened:
			Bouquet (aroma):
Date bottled:			Flavour:
			Alcohol (light/med/strong):

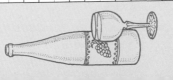

61

Name of wine:	Main ingredients:	Honey used:	Remarks:
Date yeast added:		Sugar:	
Date wine stored:			
Date clear:	Chemicals:	Final colour:	Date first bottle opened:
			Bouquet (aroma):
Date bottled:			Flavour:
			Alcohol (light/med/strong):

62

Name of wine:	Main ingredients:	Honey used:	Remarks:
Date yeast added:		Sugar:	
Date wine stored:			Date first bottle opened:
Date clear:	Chemicals:	Final colour:	Bouquet (aroma):
Date bottled:			Flavour:
			Alcohol (light/med/strong):

63

Name of wine:	Main ingredients:	Honey used:	Remarks:
Date yeast added:		Sugar:	
Date wine stored:			
Date clear:	Chemicals:	Final colour:	Date first bottle opened:
Date bottled:			Bouquet (aroma):
			Flavour:
			Alcohol (light/med/strong):

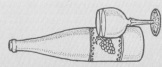

64

Fruit and wine cocktails

Golden temptation

To serve two

Pure pineapple juice (chilled) – 5 fl oz (142 ml)
Pure orange juice (chilled) – 5 fl oz (142 ml)
White wine (chilled) – 5 fl oz (142 ml)
Egg white – 1

Mix together chilled wine; pineapple and orange juice. Pour into long glasses. Whisk egg white until fluffy, then float on surface of cocktail. Sip through a straw.

Red devil

To serve two

Red wine – 5 fl oz (142 ml)
Pure blackcurrant juice – 4 fl oz (113 ml) *or*
Mineral water – 4 fl oz (113 ml) *or*
Soda water – 4 fl oz (113 ml)
Pure honey – 2 level (5 ml) teaspoons
Cherries, stones removed – 6

Mix ingredients thoroughly. Serve in long glasses. Add cherries on cocktail sticks as an attractive decoration.

Eden promise

To serve two

Pure passionfruit juice (chilled) – 5 fl oz (142 ml)
Pure pineapple juice (chilled) – 5 fl oz (142 ml)
White wine (chilled) – 5 fl oz (142 ml)
Natural yogurt (chilled) – 5 fl oz (142 ml)

Mix and blend chilled wine; passionfruit and pineapple juice. Pour into long glasses; float yogurt on surface. Drink through a straw.

Autumn kiss

To serve two

Pure apple juice (chilled) – 5 fl oz (142 ml)
Pure white grape juice (chilled) – 5 fl oz (142 ml)
Red wine – 5 fl oz (142 ml)
Pure honey – 2 level (5 ml) teaspoons
Green grapes, seedless – 6

Mix ingredients until well blended, then serve in large glasses. Add grapes on cocktail sticks as an appetizing eye-catcher.

Elderflower champagne

Sparkling wine. About 9.5% alcohol by volume.

To make 1 gallon (4½ litres)
Fresh elderflowers – 2 pints (1¼ litres) or
dried elderflowers – 2 oz (56 g)
Pure acacia blossom honey – 1 lb (454 g)
Pure white grape juice – 3½ pints (2 litres) or
concentrated white winemaking grape juice – 1 pint (568 ml)
Sultanas – 9 oz (255 g)
Lemons – 2
Strong brewed tea – ½ teacup or
winemaking grape tannin – 15 drops
Wine yeast – amount recommended by manufacturer
Water – to 1 gallon (4½ litres)

Sterilize and rinse equipment (see page 8). Dissolve honey in 1 pint (568 ml) of simmering water. Cover and leave to cool. Brew tea, allow to cool. Rinse fresh elderflowers in cold water. Rinse sultanas in colander under running warm water. Chop or mince sultanas. Extract juice from lemons; discard peel, pith and pips. Pour cool dissolved honey, tea or grape tannin, grape juice and lemon juice into plastic (food grade) bucket. Add elderflowers, sultanas, wine yeast and cold water to raise the total quantity of liquid to about 7 pints (4 litres); cover. Keep in a warm place, about 18°C (64°F) for seven days. Stir twice daily.

After seven days Pour or scoop the fermenting wine from its sediment and strain into a 1 gallon (4½ litre) demijohn; top up to the neck with cold water. Discard strained solids. Fit bung and air lock filled with water, or sulphite solution (see page 7). Leave in the warm until fermentation is complete. Fermentation has finished when bubbles have ceased passing through the liquid in the air lock; when your wine tastes dry (non-sweet); is not fizzy on your tongue; and is beginning to fall clear from the surface downwards. When satisfied fermentation has ended, rack wine (see page 40) from its sediment into a sterilized, rinsed 1 gallon (4½ litre) vessel and top up to the neck with cold water. Add a crushed Campden tablet (optional); fit a cork or rubber bung. Store somewhere cool to clear and mature before converting to sparkling wine.

Your elderflower champagne should be clear and ready for conversion to sparkling wine about three months after being stored to mature. Refer to 'How to make wine sparkle' on pages 68–69.

Sparkling gooseberry

Delightful light sparkling wine. About 9.5% alcohol by volume.

To make 1 gallon (4½ litres)

Green gooseberries – 1 lb (454 g)
Pure mixed blossom honey – 8 oz (227 g)
Pure white grape juice – 1¾ pints (1 litre)
or
concentrated white winemaking grape
juice – ½ pint (284 ml)
Sultanas – 4 oz (113 g)
Granulated sugar (optional, see below) –
14 oz (397 g)
Oranges – 2, medium sized
Strong brewed tea – ½ teacup *or*
winemaking grape tannin – 15 drops
Wine yeast – amount recommended by
manufacturer
Water – to 1 gallon (4½ litres)

Sugar free! To replace all granulated sugar (sucrose) with natural sugar (fructose and glucose) contained in natural ingredients (see page 5) miss out granulated sugar; instead *add* 1¾ pints (1 litre) extra pure white grape juice *or* ½ pint (284 ml) concentrated white winemaking grape juice and 8 oz (227 g) extra pure mixed blossom honey.

Sterilize and rinse equipment (see page 8). Dissolve granulated sugar (if used) and/or honey in 2 pints (1¼ litres) simmering water. Cover; leave to cool. Brew tea, allow to cool. Rinse gooseberries in cold water; place in plastic (food grade) bucket and mash. Cover bucket. Rinse sultanas in colander under running warm water. Chop or mince sultanas. Extract juice from oranges. Pour cool dissolved sugar and/or honey, tea or grape tannin, grape juice and orange juice into bucket. Add sultanas, wine yeast and cold water to raise total liquid to about 7 pints (4 litres); cover. Keep in warm for seven days. Stir twice daily.

After seven days Strain fermenting wine into 1 gallon (4½ litre) demijohn; top up to neck with cold water. Discard solids. Fit bung and air lock filled with water, or sulphite solution (see page 7). Leave in warm until fermentation is complete. Fermentation has finished when bubbles have ceased passing through liquid in the air lock; when your wine tastes dry (non-sweet); is not fizzy on your tongue, and is beginning to fall clear from the surface downwards. When satisfied fermentation has ceased, rack wine (see page 40) from its sediment into sterilized, rinsed 1 gallon (4½ litre) vessel; top up to neck with cold water. Add crushed Campden tablet (optional); fit cork or rubber bung. Store somewhere cool.

Your gooseberry wine should be clear and ready for conversion to sparkling wine about three months after being stored to mature. Refer to 'How to make wine sparkle' on pages 68–69

How to make wine sparkle

When the gallon (4½ litres) of wine you wish to make sparkle is clear and ready for bottling, collect six used champagne bottles, or eight 1 pint (568 ml) homebrew beer bottles, and suitable cork or plastic stoppers, or beer bottle caps.

Ordinary wine or beer bottles might not withstand the high pressure of carbon dioxide gas formed in sparkling wine and could explode – causing serious injury.

Pour or syphon ½ pint (284 ml) of the wine into a sterilized, rinsed 1 pint (568 ml) bottle. Following the manufacturer's instructions, add enough *champagne yeast* to ferment 1 gallon (4½ litres) of wine. Plug with cotton wool.

Dissolve 3 oz (85 g) of pure honey *or* 2½ oz (70 g) of granulated sugar in ¼ pint (142 ml) of boiling water; cover and leave to cool. When cool, add to the 1 pint (568 ml) bottle; plug with cotton wool. Keep in a warm place until the yeast is active and your diluted wine is bubbling; usually about twenty-four hours. Then remove ¼ pint (142 ml) of wine from your gallon (4½ litre) vessel and set aside for drinking or cooking. Pour the fermenting wine from the bottle into your gallon (4½ litre) vessel and fit a bung and air lock filled with water or sulphite solution (see page 7). Store in a warm place for twenty-four hours. Then rack fermenting wine (see page 40) into sterilized, rinsed bottles and fit stoppers or caps. Ordinary cork or plastic stoppers fitted into champagne bottles should be wired down. Special champagne stoppers and wire cages are available from homebrew stockists.

Stand the bottles in a warm place for seven days, then move somewhere cool. Store for three to four months before serving.

Always serve sparkling wine cold. Never open the bottle near your face, and point the bottle away from guests! Pour carefully, there will be some sediment at the bottom.

Sparkling summer cups

Sparkling wine makes thirst-quenching and revitalizing summer cups.

Sun tiger

To serve one

Half fill a large glass with crushed ice. Add a measure of brandy and top up with sparkling wine.

Venetian blind

To serve one

Half fill a large glass with crushed ice. Add a (5 ml) teaspoon of lemon juice; a dash of lime juice; a measure of vodka and top up with sparkling wine.

Summer snowman

To serve one

Quarter fill a long glass with crushed ice. Add 1 fl oz (28 ml) of lime juice; 2 fl oz (56 ml) of mineral water and top up to within 1½ inches (38 mm) of the mouth with sparkling wine. Float a large dollop of ice cream on the surface. Sip through a straw.

Orange cooler

To serve one

Quarter fill a long glass with crushed ice; half fill glass with pure orange juice and top up with sparkling wine.

Sparkling party punch

To serve eight to ten

Bottle sparkling wine, cold – 1
Mineral water, chilled – 1 pint (568 ml) *or*
soda water, chilled – 1 pint (568 ml)
Pure pineapple juice, chilled – 1¾ pints (1 litre)
Raspberries – ½ lb (227 g) *or*
strawberries – ½ lb (227 g)
Pure honey – 2 level tablespoons
Ice cubes – 12

Wash raspberries or strawberries in cold water; remove stalks and any diseased parts. Place all ingredients *except sparkling wine* in a large bowl and mix well. Cover and leave for 20 minutes. Then add cold sparkling wine, stir and serve in chilled glasses with a helping of fruit in each glass.

Summer punch bowl

To serve ten to twelve

Bottle white sparkling wine, cold – 1
Bottle rosé wine, chilled – 1
Pure orange juice, chilled – 1¾ pints (1 litre)
Vodka – 5 fl oz (142 ml)
Lemon, thinly sliced – 1
Ice cubes – 12

Place all ingredients *except sparkling wine* in a large bowl and mix well. Cover and leave for twenty minutes. Then add cold sparkling wine, stir and serve in chilled glasses.

Druid's mead

Delicious dry after-dinner beverage. To sweeten, see page 37. Golden colour. About 12% alcohol by volume.

To make 1 gallon (4½ litres)

Pure clover honey – 2 lb (907 g)
Pure white grape juice – 1¾ pints (1 litre)
or
concentrated white winemaking grape juice – ½ pint (284 ml)
Sultanas – 4 oz (113 g)
Lemons – 2
Orange – 1, medium sized
Strong brewed tea – ½ teacup or winemaking grape tannin – 15 drops
Wine yeast – amount recommended by manufacturer
Water – to 1 gallon (4½ litres)

Sterilize and rinse equipment (see page 8). Dissolve honey in 2 pints (1¼ litres) of simmering water. Cover and leave to cool. Brew tea, allow to cool. Rinse sultanas in colander under running warm water. Chop or mince sultanas. Extract juice from lemons and orange; discard peel, pith and pips. Pour cool dissolved honey, tea or grape tannin, grape juice, lemon and orange juice into plastic (food grade) bucket. Add sultanas, wine yeast and cold water to raise the total quantity of liquid to around 7 pints (4 litres); cover. Keep in a warm place, around 18°C (64°F) for seven days. Stir twice daily.

After seven days Pour or scoop the fermenting mead from its sediment and strain into a 1 gallon (4½ litre) demijohn; top up to the neck with cold water. Discard strained solids. Fit bung and air lock filled with water, or sulphite solution (see page 7). Leave in the warm until fermentation is complete. Fermentation has finished when bubbles have ceased passing through the liquid in the air lock; when your mead tastes dry (non-sweet); is not fizzy on your tongue, and is beginning to fall clear from the surface downwards. When satisfied fermentation has ended, rack mead (see page 40) from its sediment into a sterilized, rinsed 1 gallon (4½ litre) vessel and top up to the neck with cold water. Add a crushed Campden tablet (optional); fit a cork or rubber bung. Store somewhere cool to clear and mature before bottling (see page 49).

Your Druid's mead should be clear and ready to bottle about seven months after being stored to mature. Ready to drink two months after being bottled.

Saxon melomel

An ancient and once popular country drink, melomel is a mixture of fruit juice and honey. Saxon melomel develops a rich rosé colour and may be enjoyed as a rosé table wine or after-dinner beverage. About 10% alcohol by volume.

To make 1 gallon (4½ litres)

Pure acacia blossom honey – 1½ lb (680 g)
Pure blackcurrant juice – 1 pint (568 ml)
Raisins – 8 oz (227 g)
Lemons – 2
Strong brewed tea – ½ teacup or winemaking grape tannin – 15 drops
Wine yeast – amount recommended by manufacturer
Water – to 1 gallon (4½ litres)

Sterilize and rinse equipment (see page 8). Dissolve honey in 2 pints (1¼ litres) of simmering water. Cover and leave to cool. Brew tea, allow to cool. Rinse raisins in colander under running warm water. Chop or mince raisins. Extract juice from lemons; discard peel, pith and pips. Pour cool dissolved honey, tea or grape tannin, blackcurrant juice and lemon juice into plastic (food grade) bucket. Add raisins, wine yeast and cold water to raise the total quantity of liquid to about 7 pints (4 litres); cover. Keep in a warm place, around 18°C (64°F) for seven days. Stir twice daily.

After seven days Pour or scoop the fermenting melomel from its sediment and strain into a 1 gallon (4½ litre) demijohn; top up to the neck with cold water. Discard strained solids. Fit bung and air lock filled with water, or sulphite solution (see page 7). Leave in the warm until fermentation is complete. Fermentation has finished when bubbles have ceased passing through the liquid in the air lock; when your melomel tastes dry (non-sweet); is not fizzy on your tongue; and is beginning to fall clear from the surface downwards. When satisfied fermentation has ended, rack melomel (see page 40) from its sediment into a sterilized, rinsed 1 gallon (4½ litre) vessel and top up to the neck with cold water. Add a crushed Campden tablet (optional); fit a cork or rubber bung. Store somewhere cool to clear and mature before bottling (see page 49).

Your Saxon melomel should be clear and ready to bottle about five months after being stored to mature. Ready to drink two months after being bottled.

Celtic metheglin

Metheglin, a blend of herbs and honey, was made as an appetizing medicine by the Celts of pre-Saxon Britain. Pleasant apéritif, or after-dinner drink. About 9.5% alcohol by volume.

To make 1 gallon (4½ litres)

Dried fennel seeds – 2 oz (56 g)
Fresh or dried bay leaves – 12
Pure mixed blossom honey – 1½ lb (680 g)
Pure white grape juice – 1¾ pints (1 litre) or
concentrated white winemaking grape juice – ½ pint (284 ml)
Sultanas – 12 oz (340 g)
Oranges – 3, medium sized
Strong brewed tea – ½ teacup or
winemaking grape tannin – 15 drops
Wine yeast – amount recommended by manufacturer
Water – to 1 gallon (4½ litres)

Sterilize and rinse equipment (see page 8). Dissolve honey in 2 pints (1¾ litres) of simmering water. Cover and leave to cool. Brew tea, allow to cool. Rinse fresh bay leaves in cold water. Rinse sultanas in colander under running warm water. Chop or mince sultanas. Extract juice from oranges; discard peel, pith and pips. Pour cool dissolved honey, tea or grape tannin, grape juice and orange juice into plastic (food grade) bucket. Add fennel seeds, bay leaves, sultanas, wine yeast and cold water to raise the total quantity of liquid to about 7 pints (4 litres); cover. Keep in a warm place, around 18°C (64°F), for seven days. Stir twice daily.

After seven days Pour or scoop the fermenting metheglin from its sediment and strain into a 1 gallon (4½ litre) demijohn; top up to the neck with cold water. Discard strained solids. Fit bung and air lock filled with water, or sulphite solution (see page 7). Leave in the warm until fermentation is complete. Fermentation has finished when bubbles have ceased passing through the liquid in the air lock; when your metheglin tastes dry (non-sweet); is not fizzy on your tongue, and is beginning to fall clear from the surface downwards. When satisfied fermentation has ended, rack metheglin (see page 40) from its sediment into a sterilized, rinsed 1 gallon (4½ litre) vessel and top up to the neck with cold water. Add a crushed Campden tablet (optional); fit a cork or rubber bung. Store somewhere cool to clear and mature before bottling (see page 49).

Your Celtic metheglin should be clear and ready to bottle about five months after being stored to mature. Ready to drink two months after being bottled.

Name of wine:	Main ingredients:	Honey used:	Remarks:
Date yeast added:		Sugar:	
Date wine stored:			
			Date first bottle opened:
Date clear:	Chemicals:	Final colour:	Bouquet (aroma):
			Flavour:
Date bottled:			
			Alcohol (light/med/strong):

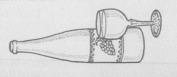

73

Name of wine:

Main ingredients:

Honey used:

Remarks:

Date yeast added:

Sugar:

Date wine stored:

Date clear:

Chemicals:

Final colour:

Date bottled:

Date first bottle opened:

Bouquet (aroma):

Flavour:

Alcohol (light/med/strong):

Name of wine:	Main ingredients:	Honey used:	Remarks:
Date yeast added:		Sugar:	
Date wine stored:			
Date clear:	Chemicals:	Final colour:	Date first bottle opened:
			Bouquet (aroma):
Date bottled:			Flavour:
			Alcohol (light/med/strong):

Name of wine:	Main ingredients:	Honey used:	Remarks:
Date yeast added:		Sugar:	
Date wine stored:			
Date clear:	Chemicals:	Final colour:	Date first bottle opened:
Date bottled:			Bouquet (aroma):
			Flavour:
			Alcohol (light/med/strong):

Name of wine:	Main ingredients:	Honey used:	Remarks:
		Sugar:	
Date yeast added:			
Date wine stored:			
			Date first bottle opened:
Date clear:	Chemicals:	Final colour:	Bouquet (aroma):
			Flavour:
Date bottled:			Alcohol (light/med/strong):

77

Name of wine:	Main ingredients:	Honey used:	Remarks:
Date yeast added:		Sugar:	
Date wine stored:			
			Date first bottle opened:
Date clear:	Chemicals:	Final colour:	Bouquet (aroma):
			Flavour:
Date bottled:			Alcohol (light/med/strong):

Name of wine:	Main ingredients:	Honey used:	Remarks:
		Sugar:	
Date yeast added:			
Date wine stored:			Date first bottle opened:
Date clear:	Chemicals:	Final colour:	Bouquet (aroma):
Date bottled:			Flavour:
			Alcohol (light/med/strong):

79

Name of wine:

Main ingredients:

Honey used:

Remarks:

Date yeast added:

Sugar:

Date wine stored:

Date clear:

Chemicals:

Final colour:

Date bottled:

Date first bottle opened:

Bouquet (aroma):

Flavour:

Alcohol (light/med/strong):

Wine vinegar

Wine vinegar tastes extra special when made from your own natural fruit or flower wines.

To make 1 pint (568 ml)

Wine (of your choice) – 10 fl oz (284 ml)
Commercial wine vinegar or malt vinegar – 5 fl oz (142 ml)
Water, cold – 5 fl oz (142 ml)

Mix ingredients together and pour into a litre bottle or three-quarter fill a large jar. Allow plenty of air space to assist full conversion into vinegar. Plug top of bottle with cotton wool or cover jar with clean muslin, nylon or cloth, and secure with an elastic band or string. Store in a warm place for eight weeks; then syphon or pour the vinegar into a saucepan and pasteurize by simmering (not boiling) for three minutes. Remove from heat, cover and allow to cool. Then re-heat until warm, about 60°C (140°F), and pour through a funnel into a warmed 1 pint (568 ml) bottle and fit a stopper or cap. For finest results, store your wine vinegar somewhere cool for seven to ten weeks to mature before using.

Vinegar with herbs

After the vinegar has matured, you may like to add crushed fresh or dried herbs to give even more flavour to your natural wine vinegar. Superb vinegars are made by infusing the flavour of herbs such as basil, coriander, borage, dill, fennel, marjoram, mint or tarragon.

One heaped tablespoon (15 ml) of fresh herbs or one heaped (5 ml) teaspoon of dried herbs is sufficient to flavour one pint (568 ml) of wine vinegar.

Method

Wash fresh herbs in warm water; crush and place in a screw top jar. Dried herbs may be put straight into the jar (crush seeds). Fill jar with wine vinegar and fasten screw top. Store in a cool place for nine days. Stir once daily.

After nine days strain vinegar back into its sterilized, rinsed bottle and fit stopper or cap. Leave for seventeen days for flavours to blend before use.

Remember to clean, sterilize and rinse *all* utensils and winemaking equipment that comes in contact with vinegar *immediately*, or subsequent wines might be infected by vinegar bacteria and begin conversion to wine vinegar.

Recipes for the festive season

Christmas punch

To serve four to six

Bottle of red or white wine – 1
Pure honey – 1 level tablespoon
Cloves, whole – 5
Nutmeg, ground – 1 level (5 ml) teaspoon
Lemon – 1
Orange – 1

Extract juice from lemon and orange. Discard pith, pips and orange peel. Cut lemon peel into thin strips and place in large saucepan. Add juice from lemon and orange; honey, cloves, nutmeg and the wine. Stir and heat gently until punch is hot and starting to simmer. Then remove from heat, cover and allow to cool for two or three minutes before straining into warmed glasses. Drink while hot.

Wassail 'good health' bowl

To serve six to eight

Bottles of red or white wine – 1½
Cooking apples – 3, large
Pure honey – 2 level tablespoons
Raisins – 4 oz (113 g)
Ground ginger – 3 level (5 ml) teaspoons
Ground cinnamon – 1 level (5 ml) teaspoon
Water – ½ pint (284 ml)

Wash and quarter apples; remove and discard cores and peel. Chop apples into small chunks and simmer in ½ pint (284 ml) of water until soft. Remove from heat. Mash apple in water, cover. Pour wine into separate large saucepan. Add honey, raisins, ginger and cinnamon. Stir and heat gently until simmering. Then remove from heat and cover. Pour the mashed apple into a punch bowl (or any suitable bowl). Add wine mixture, stir and serve immediately in heated glasses.

Fruit punch

To serve four to six

Bottle of red or white wine – 1
Pineapple chunks – 8 oz (227 g)
Mandarin oranges – 4 oz (113 g)
Pure honey – 1 level tablespoon

Pour wine, fruit and juice (from tinned fruit) into a large saucepan. Add honey and stir over low heat until beginning to simmer; then ladle into warmed glasses and serve straight away.

Caudle

To serve two to three

Bitter beer – 2 pints (1.13 litres)
Pure honey – 2 level tablespoons
Porridge oats – 1 level tablespoon
Nutmeg, ground – 2 level (5 ml) teaspoons
Lemon – 1

Cut washed lemon into thin slices; put slices aside. Pour beer into a large saucepan. Add oats and nutmeg, Stir in honey and warm mixture over low heat until simmering; then remove from heat and cover. Leave the caudle to cool for two to three minutes, then strain into warmed tankards or glasses and float a slice or two of lemon in each tankard or glass.

Bishop

To serve four to six

Bottle of red or white wine – 1
Oranges, large – 2
Pure honey – 2 heaped tablespoons

Wash oranges; cut and split each *unpeeled* orange half-way down its centre. Put in an open casserole dish and place one heaped tablespoon of honey in the split middle of each orange. Bake in preheated moderate oven, gas Mark 4 (350° F) for twenty minutes. Then tip baked oranges and juice into a large saucepan. Add wine and heat gently until simmering, then remove from heat and cover. Leave to cool for two to three minutes; then strain bishop into warmed glasses. The oranges, when cool, may be sliced and the juicy flesh sucked from the peel.

Saxon ale versus British beer

'Real ale' is very different from today's hopped beer. Ale was the favourite drink of the Anglo-Saxons. It was brewed from barley and flavoured with honey, flowers, fruit and herbs. There were dozens of different styles of ale; each providing a vital daily intake of vitamins and minerals. Ale was a powerful package of natural goodness and its health-bestowing and healing qualities were fully appreciated by Anglo-Saxon settlers.

Saxon ale was brewed mainly for warriors. Surviving recipes show the final alcoholic strength of Saxon ale was probably higher than many of our commercial table wines. It was diluted with water for those with weaker heads!

Our 'beer' is a Dutch drink, brought to England in the sixteenth century by Dutch Protestant refugees fleeing from the Netherlands to escape religious persecution.

Beer was brewed from barley, but was far weaker than English ale; so low in flavour and alcohol that hops were added to lend beer taste and prevent beer from fast turning to vinegar. Hops are a natural antiseptic; however, they are also a soporific.

Unlike English ale, which was powerful, vitalizing and invigorating, Dutch beer was weak, watery and sleep-inducing. In fact 'beer' was a joke among the English for over a hundred years, before its easy and economical large-scale production became necessary to produce an adequate supply for the fast growing and always thirsty population.

Today's 'real ales' are hopped beer, not real ale at all. British commercial pub beer is more expensive and lower in malt, hops and alcohol than ever before in English history.

The only way we can sample some of the lost English ales or enjoy a traditional pint of British beer, is to make our own, at a fraction of the price we would expect to pay over a bar.

There is nothing finer than savouring a pint of your own home-brewed Shakespearean 'sack' (barley, fennel, honey and rue); Saxon honey ale; fruit ales; Elizabethan herb and spice ales; or highly nutritious home-brewed traditional beers, lagers and stouts.

You can also make your own unique English ale, malt vinegars and traditional warming winter punches.

Equipment

To make 1 gallon (4½ litres) of ale or beer, you need:

1 One 2¼ (10 litre) plastic (food grade) bucket with lid.
2 Eight 1 pint (568 ml) homebrew beer bottles with plastic or metal caps.

Cooking with ale

Home-brewed ale, beer and lager can be used in wholesome home cooking in exactly the same way as wine to brighten the appetizing appeal and enrich the flavour of casseroles, marinades, gravies, poached fish, pot roasts, sauces, soups and stews.

Best British bitter

Best British beer is made the way beer ought to be brewed – wholly from pure malt, without added sugar (sucrose). About 4.5% alcohol by volume.

To make 1 gallon (4½ litres)

*Pure malt extract syrup – 1¼ lbs (567 g)
Dried hops – 1 oz (28 g)
**Cracked crystal malt grains – 2 oz (56 g)
Beer yeast – amount recommended by manufacturer
Water – to 1 gallon (4½ litres)

*1 lb (454 g) of pure malt extract syrup contains about 12 oz (340 g) of natural malt sugar (maltose).
**Cracked crystal malt grains are available from your homebrew stockist.

Sterilize and rinse equipment (see page 8). Pour pure malt extract syrup into large saucepan. Add about 4 pints (2¼ litres) of water. Switch on low heat and raise gently to a simmer – stirring until the malt syrup dissolves. Add cracked crystal malt grains and half the total measure of dried hops. Stir hops into liquid; cover the saucepan and simmer for twenty minutes. Then add remaining half of hops. Stir well, cover and simmer for a further ten minutes. Then turn off heat and allow to cool. During this cooling phase the full hop flavour and goodness is absorbed into your brew.

When cool Pour or scoop liquid and strain into a plastic (food grade) bucket. Discard strained solids. Add beer yeast and cold water to raise the total quantity of liquid to 1 gallon (4½ litres). Cover bucket and remove to a warm place, around 18°C (64°F). Leave your beer undisturbed for seven days to ferment.

After seven days Check to see if fermentation has finished. It will have finished when frothing has stopped; bubbling has ceased, and the beer's surface is still. The beer should taste dry (non-sweet) and not fizzy on your tongue. The previously cloudy beer will be clearing from the surface downwards.

When satisfied your beer has finished fermenting, prime and bottle (see page 40).

Your best British bitter is ready to enjoy twenty-one days from being bottled, but is 'best' after seven weeks in bottles.

Anglo-Saxon ale

This is *real* ale. It is strong and full of flavour. About 6% alcohol by volume.

To make 1 gallon (4½ litres)

*Pure malt extract syrup – 1 lb (454 g)
Pure apple juice – ½ pint (284 ml)
Pure mixed blossom honey – 8 oz (227 g)
Dried borage – 1 oz (28 g)
Beer yeast – amount recommended by manufacturer
Water – to 1 gallon (4½ litres)

*1lb (454 g) of pure malt extract syrup contains about 12 oz (340 g) of natural malt sugar (maltose).

Sterilize and rinse equipment (see page 8). Pour pure malt extract syrup into a large saucepan. Add about 4 pints (2¼ litres) of water. Switch on low heat and raise gently to a simmer – stirring until the malt syrup dissolves. Add half the total measure of dried borage. Stir borage into liquid; cover the saucepan and simmer for twenty minutes. Then add remaining half of borage and all the pure honey. Stir well, cover and simmer for a further ten minutes. Then turn off heat and allow to cool. During this cooling phase the full borage flavour and goodness is absorbed into your brew.

When cool pour or scoop liquid and strain into a plastic (food grade) bucket. Discard strained solids. Add pure apple juice, beer yeast and cold water to raise the total quantity of liquid to 1 gallon (4½ litres). Cover bucket and remove to a warm place, about 18°C (64°F). Leave your ale undisturbed for seven days to ferment.

After seven days Check to see if fermentation has finished. It will have finished when frothing has stopped; bubbling ceased, and the ale's surface is still. The ale should taste dry (non-sweet) and not fizzy on your tongue. The previously cloudy ale will be clearing from the surface downwards.

When satisfied your ale has finished fermenting, prime and bottle (see page 40).

Your Anglo-Saxon ale is ready to enjoy twenty-eight days from being bottled, but is greatly improved after eight weeks in bottles.

Bottling and serving beer

When satisfied your ale or beer has finished fermenting (see recipes) assemble eight homebrew beer bottles for each gallon (4½ litres) of brew you wish to bottle. Sterilize and rinse bottles (see page 8) and snap-on plastic caps or metal caps. If using metal caps, you will need a special capping tool, available from your homebrew stockist, to crimp the metal caps firmly in place.

Priming

Next, prime the brew by adding dissolved pure malt extract syrup to your fermented ale or beer. Natural malt sugar (maltose) in the priming malt is fermented in the sealed bottles by still active beer yeast; supplying sparkle and a protective layer of carbon dioxide gas to guard against bacterial infection.

Method

Dissolve two level tablespoons of pure malt extract syrup in ¼ pint (142 ml) of boiling water for each gallon (4½ litres) of brew you wish to prime. Cover and allow to cool. When cool, pour into a bucket of fermented brew and stir carefully to avoid disturbing too much the thick layer of beer yeast sediment at the bucket bottom. Cover and leave for ten minutes to settle. Then scoop some brew into a jug and fill bottles through a sterilized, rinsed plastic funnel or syphon brew into bottles with a plastic syphon tube as you would when winemaking (see page 40). Fill each bottle to within 1 inch (25 mm) of its mouth. When you have filled the bottles, fasten the caps.

Storing

Label your capped bottles and store somewhere warm, about 18°C (64°F) for seven days; then move to a cool place to condition and mature until ready for enjoyable drinking (see recipes for suggested storage period).

Serving

Bitter beer should be served cool, not chilled. Serve Anglo-Saxon ale (recipe on page 87) and light ales chilled.

When pouring ale or beer into a glass, keep the bottle at an angle so sediment stays at the bottom of your bottle. Steadily trickle the ale or beer down the inside of your glass to reduce frothing. Stop pouring when sediment appears.

Ale and bitter beer complement red meat dishes (particularly beef); salads rich in flavour and dressing; traditional British fish and chip suppers, and the English ploughman's lunch of crusty wholemeal rolls and tasty cheese.

Name of wine:	Main ingredients:	Honey used:	Remarks:
		Sugar:	
Date yeast added:			
Date wine stored:			
			Date first bottle opened:
Date clear:	Chemicals:	Final colour:	Bouquet (aroma):
			Flavour:
Date bottled:			Alcohol (light/med/strong):

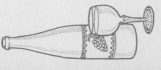

Name of wine:	Main ingredients:	Honey used:	Remarks:
Date yeast added:		Sugar:	
Date wine stored:			
Date clear:	Chemicals:	Final colour:	Date first bottle opened:
			Bouquet (aroma):
Date bottled:			Flavour:
			Alcohol (light/med/strong):

Name of wine:

Main ingredients:

Honey used:

Remarks:

Date yeast added:

Sugar:

Date wine stored:

Date clear:

Chemicals:

Final colour:

Date first bottle opened:

Date bottled:

Bouquet (aroma):

Flavour:

Alcohol (light/med/strong):

Name of wine:	Main ingredients:	Honey used:	Remarks:
Date yeast added:		Sugar:	
Date wine stored:			
			Date first bottle opened:
Date clear:	Chemicals:	Final colour:	Bouquet (aroma):
Date bottled:			Flavour:
			Alcohol (light/med/strong):

Name of wine:	Main ingredients:	Honey used:	Remarks:
Date yeast added:		Sugar:	
Date wine stored:			
Date clear:	Chemicals:	Final colour:	Date first bottle opened:
			Bouquet (aroma):
Date bottled:			Flavour:
			Alcohol (light/med/strong):

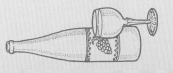

93

Name of wine:	Main ingredients:	Honey used:	Remarks:
Date yeast added:		Sugar:	
Date wine stored:			Date first bottle opened:
Date clear:	Chemicals:	Final colour:	Bouquet (aroma):
Date bottled:			Flavour:
			Alcohol (light/med/strong):

Name of wine:	Main ingredients:	Honey used:	Remarks:
		Sugar:	
Date yeast added:			
Date wine stored:			
	Chemicals:	Final colour:	Date first bottle opened:
Date clear:			Bouquet (aroma):
Date bottled:			Flavour:
			Alcohol (light/med/strong):

Name of wine:

Main ingredients:

Honey used:

Remarks:

Date yeast added:

Sugar:

Date wine stored:

Date clear:

Chemicals:

Final colour:

Date bottled:

Date first bottle opened:

Bouquet (aroma):

Flavour:

Alcohol (light/med/strong):

Acknowledgements
Drawings: Lorna Turpin
Photography: Oliver Hunter
96 Winemaking equipment supplied by courtesy of Boots The Chemist.